CAPTAIN AMERICA

DARK DESIGNS

CAPTAIN AMERICA

DARK DESIGNS

MARVEL

CAPTAIN AMERICA: DARK DESIGNS PROSE NOVEL. Published by MARVEL WORLDWIDE, INC., a subsidiary of MARVEL ENTERTAINMENT, LLC. OFFICE OF PUBLICATION: 135 West 50th Street, New York, NY 10020. Copyright © 2016 MARVEL

ISBN# 978-0-7851-9985-4

Printed in the U.S.A.

ALAN FINE, President, Marvel Entertainment; DAN BUCKLEY, President, TV, Publishing and Brand Management; JOE QUESADA, Chief Creative Officer; TOM BREVOORT, SVP of Publishing; DAVID BOGART, SVP of Operations & Procurement, Publishing; C.B. CEBULSKI, VP of International Development & Brand Management; DAVID GABRIEL, SVP Print, Sales & Marketing; DAN CARR, Executive Director of Publishing Technology; SUSAN CRESPI, Editorial Operations Manager; ALEX MORALES, Publishing Operations Manager; STAN LEE, Chairman Emeritus. For information regarding advertising in Marvel Comics or on Marvel.com, please contact Jonathan Rheingold, VP of Custom Solutions & Ad Sales, at jrheingold@marvel.com. For Marvel subscription inquiries, please call 800-217-9158. **Manufactured between 2/12/2016 and 3/21/2016 by SHERIDAN, CHELSEA, MI, USA.**

First printing 2016
10 9 8 7 6 5 4 3 2 1

Cover art by Steve McNiven, Jay Leisten, and Justin Ponsor
Interior art by Steve Epting, Jackson Guice, Michael Lark, Jay Leisten, Steve McNiven, Mike Perkins, Dexter Vines, and Patrick Zircher

Special thanks to Jeff Christiansen, Kevin Garcia, Daron Jensen, and Mike O'Sullivan

Joan Hilty and Stuart Moore, Editors
Design by Jay Bowen

VP, Production & Special Products: Jeff Youngquist
Associate Editor: Sarah Brunstad
SVP Print, Sales & Marketing: David Gabriel
Editor In Chief: Axel Alonso
Chief Creative Officer: Joe Quesada
Publisher: Dan Buckley
Executive Producer: Alan Fine

For David Marquis, a real hero who has devoted his life to bringing the joy of art to over 345,000 schoolchildren in NYC.

CAPTAIN AMERICA

DARK DESIGNS

MARVEL

*It's not about the individual. It's about the design,
the pattern.*

SUMMER, 2005. The dirt-caked vehicle bouncing along Somalia's
flat, thorn-bush savannah looked like any National Army personnel
carrier: an olive-drab truck with a canvas-covered bed. As soon as it
passed, the locals—many living in domed huts fashioned from spin-
dly branches and discarded plastic sheets—went back to their day.

They'd seen plenty.

But within the truck, surrounded by high-tech S.H.I.E.L.D.
equipment, Captain America and his two companions sat in air-
conditioned comfort. Agent Walter Jacobs scrutinized various
screens while Dr. Nia N'Tomo reviewed the notes on her PDA. The
blond, blue-eyed Steve Rogers stared out the back, watching tired
camels sip the muddy waters of the Mandera Dawa River.

Brazen sunlight accented the metallic window frame, making it
look more like an interdimensional portal than bulletproof glass. The
near-wasteland on the other side could almost have passed for an
alternate universe. Jiilaal, one of the two dry seasons, had left the
terrain arid hues of tan with patches of green few and far between.

The view made Rogers wonder whether he'd spent more time on other worlds than he had in this part of his own. National boundaries brought a different sort of danger than cosmic beings. Having been a one-man public-relations campaign during World War II, he was well aware of how complicated propaganda had grown. It'd been easier when the Nazis just thought they were superior. You could prove that wrong by defeating them in combat.

Here and now, the militant fundamentalist Al-Shabaab controlled a large area to the south. The mere presence of Steve's stars-and-stripes uniform could be spun as interference from a decadent Western colonizer, providing recruitment fodder for more troops.

Much as he loathed being seen as one of the bullies he'd spent his life fighting, he'd never wear anything else. Whenever he did right by the red, white, and blue, the principles behind it became not abstractions, but living ideals.

What had Churchill said? "You can depend upon the Americans to do the right thing. But only after they've exhausted all the other possibilities."

He smiled at the wry critique. After all, the British Bulldog also said democracy was the worst possible form of government—except for all the others.

As humans, Rogers thought, all we can ever do is strive.

The view gave way to a smattering of trees with bone-skinny trunks that seemed too frail to hold their heavy tops. He'd been frail himself once, near death as a sickly child, but who would believe that now? In time, any desert might become a paradise.

Ahead lay a few stone structures clustered near a rare power line. When the driver veered west, Cap felt relieved. Propaganda aside, when it came to stopping a bacteriological bomb, fewer witnesses also meant fewer possible victims.

As the buildings shrank into the distance, a beep from the sensor array turned him back to the truck's dark interior. "Jacobs?"

The glow from the readout gave the red-haired agent's sunburnt skin a blue-white hue. "I've got a 98 percent confidence match with the signature of an Al-Hussein Scud missile a half-mile off."

Frowning, Dr. N'Tomo slumped against the canvas sidewall. "With a 400-mile range, that could hit a number of Wakandan population centers, even if they don't know what they're aiming for. I... was right."

Being stewards of the world's only source of Vibranium, a metal with an uncanny ability to absorb kinetic energy, made the tribal nation of Wakanda vastly wealthy—and a target. Rogers understood more than most why a large portion of its wealth was spent keeping its exact location a secret. His shield was fashioned from an accidental combination of Vibranium and an iron alloy.

He leaned toward Dr. N'Tomo. "If it weren't for you, we'd still be back in the Helicarrier thinking this was just a bluff."

Usually poker-faced, she gave him a slight smile. The look of her brown skin and sharp eyes against the olive green of the borrowed fatigues suited her gravitas. "I'm still disappointed. In my line of work, we'd rather not be in demand."

"I hear that." Wondering how much of his own expression she could see through the mask, he gave her a casual salute. "Then here's to our early retirement."

Bringing a subject-matter expert on a military op was always a dicey proposition, but she was no lab jockey. Great-niece of Wakanda's royal champion N'Tomo, Nia N'Tomo had done plenty of her own field work with the AIDS epidemics in Swaziland and Ebola outbreaks in West Africa. They'd met for the first time on the Helicarrier, and it hadn't taken long for Rogers to recognize and admire her instincts.

"If Somali pirates can acquire a missile and a weaponized virus this easily, I doubt that will ever happen." She raised a playful eyebrow. "Speaking of free time, S.H.I.E.L.D. spirited me away from my first free day in eight months. I wouldn't mind sharing a drink when this is over."

Already finding her a tough read, Steve wasn't sure whether she was flirting or being friendly. Being an asthmatic weakling before the war and then lying for decades frozen in Arctic ice hadn't provided many opportunities for relationships.

"A drink. I...can't... I..."

Her poker face quickly returned. She *had* been flirting. "I'm sorry if I was being inappropriate."

"No, it's not that. I just metabolize alcohol too quickly for it to have any effect. A result of the Super-Soldier serum. And no one likes a drinking partner with a good memory." As he kept talking, she frowned, apparently as confused by him as he was by her. "Or so I've been told."

She studied him. After a moment, the knitted brow turned back into the slight smile.

Noticing the wry look from Jacobs, Steve quickly changed the subject. "An old Scud wouldn't be hard for anyone to find, if they've got the cash. But you can't get weaponized rabies locally. The pirates have a history of working with financiers, even more now that the international push has driven them to attempt more land operations."

"I've been too buried in rabies research to read the latest brief. Any theories yet on who?"

He shrugged. "Someone who wants Vibranium and doesn't care how they get it."

"A lot of choices, then. Still, this seems especially desperate. Even if they manage a launch, our air defense has an excellent chance of knocking it out of the sky. The real concern is if something goes wrong on the ground. The three of us have been vaccinated, but given the high cost and the lack of an actual cure, an airborne rabies epidemic would devastate the local populace, and we can't even be certain our vaccine is effective until we identify the strain."

"Which is why I'm here to neutralize any resistance while you and Jacobs secure the payload for transport—or, if possible, nullify the virus on site."

"We're expecting 15 or more armed guards. I assume you're all right with those odds?"

"Actually, it's not really fair to the guards, doctor."

This time she definitely smiled. "The name is Nia."

"Steve. And I make it a point never to disappoint a top-ten epidemiologist."

"Top five, actually, Steve."

He liked the way she said it, as if correcting poor grammar.

As the truck slowed, Jacobs cleared his throat. "As top of my class at interpreting beeps and flashing red lights, I need you both to know we're within 50 yards of the target. Are we all set to handle the virus, doctor?"

"Incineration would be best, but as long as it's still outside the human body, UV irradiation will suffice." She raised what looked like an unusually large spotlight gun. "And this provides a much more concentrated blast. If there's any sign the virus has been released, the hazmat suits are ready."

Only flat landscape was visible from the rear; Rogers shifted closer to Jacobs to check the forward view on his monitors. They'd reached the edge of a desert village: six or seven round huts, a few with thatched roofs, separated by low rock walls. With most of the inhabitants likely indoors avoiding the heat, it looked empty, save for two children leading an elderly man. They stopped to stare at the truck.

"We're out in the open. I don't like this."

Jacobs smirked. "We're in a truck on a plain with scrub grass and low bushes. Without a cloak, it's not as if we have a choice. But the idea was to keep it small—that's why you're here instead of an entire task force."

Rogers grunted agreement. "I do have the advantage of not taking up much space. Can't say the same for a missile launcher." He tapped the glass, pointing to the largest hut. "And that's the only thing in visual range big enough to hold one."

Jacobs zoomed the truck's camera toward the hut entrance. It caught a glint of something metallic in the dry darkness. "That's it. But where are the guards?"

Nia moved nearer to watch. "Inside?"

"Pull back," Rogers said. The camera returned to a wider view, but it showed only dirt and patches of low vegetation. "Those bushes. I've seen them everywhere but inside the villages. Look how they're arranged, almost as if in…"

Before Rogers could say *formation,* one of the gangly things tumbled sideways. A man—thin, but muscular—rose from the hole beneath it. Dry earth rained from the patterned scarf around his head and the RPG gripped in his hands.

Rogers headed for the rear door. "On it."

Jacobs switched on the comm; though already several feet away, Rogers could now hear Dr. N'Tomo's instructions to the driver as if they were whispered in his ear.

"Get us to that hut immediately."

As he flew through the doors, Cap said, "Belay that order. Appreciate your enthusiasm, doctor, but you'll have to keep your distance until I clear the area."

She glared at his back. "And if they launch?"

"They won't, Nia."

Before landing, he shouted to the elderly man and the children, "Run!"

His boots raised tan dust-puffs that grew into a small cloud. He rolled left, spun toward the guard, knelt and threw his shield. A hot blur of sun-drenched red, white, and blue struck the RPG in the center, splitting it in two.

Before the visual could travel the short distance from the gunman's eyes to his brain, the shield slammed into his skull. He was out. More trained meteor than boomerang, the shield returned to Rogers' waiting hand.

Less than a second had elapsed, but five more "bushes" had fallen away. Two men scrambled from the waist-deep holes. Another three stood where they were and opened fire. There was no cover, but with the shooters still in the holes, their bullets sprayed low to the ground, making them easy for Rogers to avoid. Like a quick round of whack-a-mole, another shield-toss took out all three. By then the two runners were on him, and the remaining bushes had been tossed aside.

More gunshots came his way. Missing outright or careening off his shield, they flew helter-skelter into stone walls, dirt, or sky.

Some of the guns were automatic, a few single-shot. Rogers' keen senses and hard-won experience told him what came from where. The two charging men had pistols. The ones in the holes, now too numerous for another shield strike, held the greater fire-power. Unfortunately, the rising dust made it difficult to see every weapon they carried.

The truck was bulletproof, but a second RPG could take it out. Ignoring the runners, he headed for the foxholes—until a double-check of the perimeter stopped him cold.

The old man and the children, a boy and a girl, hadn't budged. They stood there gawking, not at the gunmen, but at him. Their predictable day shattered, they were in shock. When a stray shot hit the dirt at their feet, the old man wrapped his bony arms protectively around the children, but they still didn't run.

Rogers knew he'd bring the bullets with him if he headed toward them to help. To draw the fire away, he pivoted in the opposite direction. But the truck disobeyed his orders. Gouging thick lines in the earth, it put itself between them and the gunfire.

He glimpsed Nia pulling the civilians inside the open rear doors before a groan of gears turned him back toward the large hut. The tip of a Scud, rising into launch position, poked through the thatched roof. Sunlight intruded on the dark interior, revealing the edges of an old Soviet 8x8 artillery truck, exactly the type needed to transport and launch the tactile ballistic missile.

He didn't have time to admire the two runners for being willing to face him up close. His rising shield smacked the pistol from one man's hand. An elbow to the chin knocked the other out cold. The disarmed man went to his knees and raised his hands in surrender—only to be hit by the continuing fire from the foxholes.

Throwing his shield ahead, Rogers ran toward the holes. The spinning disc took out four more of the men. Two kicks and a roundhouse eliminated another three. The last man standing whirled to face him just in time for the returning shield to clonk the back of his head.

All the weapons were automatics. The RPG was a one-off. Good.

He rushed into the hut just as the Scud locked into its firing position.

The slightly heavy man at the controls was better dressed than the others, his beard neatly groomed. One hand hovering over the launch button, he gesticulated with the other as he spoke.

"Look at you, fancy hero, U.S.A. Think that we're the bad guys? No." His English was broken, his speech slurred. "We take food from the U.N. ships before the warlords can steal it, so more people can eat. Tankers come into our waters, destroy our fishing, so we take payment."

There was something wrong with him, and it had nothing to do with the rhetoric. He was sweating. It was a desert, of course, but this man was dripping. Heat exhaustion didn't make sense. Not only would he be used to these climes, the wet canteen dangling from his side made dehydration seem unlikely.

Rogers relaxed his stance. "What's your name?"

"My name? I don't want to give you my name. Call me Robin Hood. You know him?"

"I do. So you're not the bad guy, great. How about proving it by stepping away from the missile that's threatening innocent lives?"

Robin Hood's shoulder twitched. He clenched his free fist. "It's the greedy Wakandans who are killers! They have all the Vibranium in the world. The money we could raise from the small amount we asked for could feed thousands. If they gave us that, none of this would be happening. But they needed motivation, so they will get it."

"Let's say I believe you. Do you know what your partner will do with their half? I've got a feeling they won't be using it to feed anyone."

Robin Hood grabbed at his own arm, then started punching it. A heart attack?

Nia spoke through the comm. "Those are rabies symptoms."

Still in the truck, she was watching the scene on the monitors via Cap's body cam. It was the first time he'd heard tension in her voice. "The payload is leaking?"

"Not necessarily. Rabies symptoms don't appear for two to twelve weeks following infection. I don't see any obvious signs in the gunmen or the civilians. It's more likely he was exposed while arming the missile."

The hand above the launch button wavered. If it moved away for a fraction of a second, Rogers knew he'd have the man. But when Rogers took a cautious step forward, Robin Hood rallied.

"Stay put, U.S.A."

Cap locked eyes with him. "You're infected."

Head shaking, the pirate chuckled. "I know it. Our sterilization facility was not up to Western standards. It was a storage shed. But it will be worth dying if my family won't have to worry for the rest of their lives."

"You don't have to die. We can help you." He whispered softly into the comm, "Right, Nia?"

The answer was even softer. "Uh, no. Once the neurological symptoms begin, rabies is almost always fatal. But now would not be a good time to tell him that. Known strains of the virus are transmitted through saliva, from a bite, but we're getting into our suits in case this is different. Keep your distance."

The pirate's eyes darted about. One moment he was looking toward the entrance, the next at the shadows in the hut. "What do your friends in the truck say, U.S.A.? They think they can take me out with a sniper?"

"There's no sniper, I swear. It's fine. Everything is fine. If you'll just—"

"Everything is *not* fine!" Snarling, he slammed his hand down toward the controls.

Rogers' enhanced reflexes sent the shield sailing. In an instant, the pirate's body was curled around the disc's spinning edge, flying backwards. But as he flew, the fingers of his flailing hand hit the button.

Rogers, N'Tomo, and Jacobs all shouted, "No!"

Smoke poured from the Scud's engines. Its hissing mixed with a sad, cackling laugh. Robin Hood lay on the earth, the shield still atop him.

"See?" he said between rattling coughs. "I told you everything would not be fine."

Flames pressed from the roaring rocket motor. The missile shook, but did not rise. A look at the launcher told Rogers why: Thanks to the operator's incompetence or disease, the restraining straps that kept the Scud in place for transport hadn't been disengaged.

The thrust was building. Either the metal bands would snap, releasing the missile, or it would expel its deadly cargo here and now.

As Rogers ran for his shield, he heard Nia scream. "Don't touch it! It could be contaminated."

"I need it to pry open the missile covering."

Having heard her through the comm, he didn't realize she'd left the truck until the bluish UV rays glanced along his back and shoulders. Covered head to toe by a military-grade hazmat suit, she was waving the UV gun about as if attempting to cleanse the air.

She came up alongside him. "We'll have to find another way. But if you let me get to the payload, I think I can defuse it. I *know* I can."

I know I can.

Her words, mixed with the roar and smoke, conjured a deeply ingrained memory. An eager teen in the war, clinging to a hijacked drone, had told him much the same:

I can bring the plane back—I know I can!

Let go! It might be booby-trapped! You can't deactivate the bomb without me! Drop off!

You're right, Cap! I see the fuse! It's gonna...

He wanted to shove her away for her own protection, but settled for shouting, "There's no time! Stay back!"

The few yards to the launcher seemed like a mile. Having lived with his augmented body for so long, he had a pretty good idea how strong he was. He knew, for instance, that he could push a full-sized car a yard or so sideways. But he had no idea at all whether he could do what he had in mind. He'd have to land above the engine to avoid the yellow-white flames, but he'd also need his hands free.

So he jumped, landing upside-down, and wrapped his legs around the missile's base. Even from here, the heat from the thrusters burned him through his uniform.

I don't know how Spider-Man does it...

His added weight shifted the balance. The restraints snapping, the missile tilted. Before the few remaining metal bands could give, he drove his fists through the covering, reaching toward the propellant pumps and the raging motor itself. His body offered some heat resistance, his gloves a little more, but neither stopped the searing pain as he braced his feet against the missile, wrapped his fingers around the hot engine mounts, and pulled.

He had to rip out the engine—and fast, before the fuel tank could ignite.

Once it came half free, he twisted and turned, hoping to use the suddenly unhindered thrust to steer the engine away from the body of the Scud. It roared off in a mad blur. He fell backwards, scorched by the edge of the trailing exhaust. The rest of the Scud teetered and fell. At first, he wasn't sure whether he'd succeeded. If the missile hit the ground hard enough to ignite the impact fuse at its tip, the payload would disperse.

Instead, the cylindrical body came to rest on the edge of the hut's wall, its nose pointed toward a thick cloud low on the horizon, just visible through the hole in the ceiling left by the Scud. Once he got to his feet, a gaping hole in the opposite wall told him where the engine had gone. Disconnected from its fuel source, it had petered out, the charred metal leaving a thin trail of black smoke that seemed an insult to the wide blue sky.

A happy giggle turned him back toward the entrance.

Nia was holding back one of the children, the little girl. Despite being restrained by a stranger in a hazmat suit, she was wide-eyed, grinning, saying, "Captain America!"

Oh, dying would matter to <u>them</u>, of course.
No one wants to die.

THE HOSPITAL gown was uncomfortable. Rogers had taken it off. Sitting in his white underpants on the edge of the table, he felt as if he was waiting to be examined for the draft. But it wasn't December 8, 1941, and he wasn't on New York's Lower East Side. He was about 50,000 feet up, still somewhere over Africa, he assumed, stuck in a small quarantine chamber in Lab 247 on a S.H.I.E.L.D. Helicarrier staffed by nearly two thousand personnel.

He tugged out the borrowed laptop's earbuds and looked up from the movie he'd been trying to watch. The only sound was the steady hiss of the negative air pressure, meant to prevent the spread of contagious disease. An immune system like his, enhanced by the Super-Soldier serum, provided its own substantial protection, but with the details of the weaponized virus unknown, they rightly were taking no chances.

Rogers didn't mind the boredom. He *did* mind not knowing what was going on with the others. Regardless of her hazmat suit, Nia had been close to the infected pirate. Bilan, the child who had run in to see him, had been completely unprotected.

He looked through the clear wall into the lab's whites and silvers. His sole companion, Dr. Winston Kade, moved from instrument to instrument, making notes in a PDA. If Nia had a poker face, Kade's was stone. While his expression said nothing, his appearance revealed him as a 60-something who'd survived rough times. His skin had an odd yellowish pallor. Chunks of his salt-and-pepper hair were missing in a pattern that resembled radiation burns.

Rogers didn't want to distract him from his work, but it had been hours since he'd had an update. At least they'd determined the warhead hadn't leaked, and that it wasn't likely "Robin Hood" had infected any others. Seeing their leader's corpse, the captured gunmen, fearing for their families, had cooperated freely, providing every location the virus had been. But still not who supplied it.

The film he'd been watching didn't help, but the laptop hadn't been cleared for connection to the Helicarrier network. Its current playlist belonged to its owner, Kade. Thinking Rogers would feel more at home with a black-and-white movie, he'd suggested 1950's *Panic in the Streets*, a thriller about a race to prevent a plague outbreak in New Orleans. The rest of the choices were similarly odd for someone in quarantine: *The Andromeda Strain, Crazies, Outbreak, 28 Days Later.*

Maybe he should be glad the guy wasn't talkative.

Still, Nia insisted Kade was number one in the field, that they were lucky to have him. Apparently the promise of access to some new Stark Industries med-scanner was too tempting for him to pass up.

His patience at an end, Steve rapped on the glass, but the composite was thick, the hiss of the air loud, and the distance too great. Either that, or Kade was ignoring him. He waited until the doctor passed directly in front of him, then pounded a bit harder than he intended.

The rattling stopped them both short.

"Sorry about that."

Eyes suddenly wide, Kade stepped back and checked the monitors for leaks. Satisfied, he flicked the intercom button. "Yes?"

"The children from the village, the old man—do you know yet if they're all right?"

Kade nodded. "They were cleared and returned to their homes long before we left Somali airspace."

"Nia...Dr. N'Tomo? And Agent Jacobs?"

He kept nodding. "Both cleared, as were the gunmen. The rabies was a standard strain, rather poorly aerosolized. To catch it, you'd either have to directly inhale it during the few hours it would remain viable, or be bitten by someone infected."

"That's great, but, then... I'm the only one still in isolation?"

Kade gave him a strangely quick nod, as if impatient at having to state the obvious. "Yes."

Rogers' brow knitted. "Can I ask why?"

"You're an unusual man with unusual biometrics. Unusual things warrant more scrutiny." He looked down as he spoke, fingers dancing across the PDA keys.

"Uh...anything you're not telling me, doc?"

"Yes."

Rogers expected him to continue, but Kade walked off and went back to work.

Reminded of another genius who sometimes failed to see the trees for the forest, he laughed lightly to himself. *This guy's even more distracted than Tony Stark. I guess I'll find out when I find out.*

Rather than dwell on the uneasy sensation of being treated like a lab rat, he focused on the fact that everyone else was all right— especially Nia. Finding himself a little *too* relieved about Nia's health, he turned back to the laptop.

Maybe he should give *The Crazies* a try. But he did prefer black-and-white films. There was something about the lack of color that made things seem more real.

He was about to press PLAY when the lab door opened and Nia walked in. No longer in fatigues, she wore a lab coat over her tasteful civvies. A small pendant, which he recognized as a symbol of Wakanda's N'Tomo clan, hung from her neck. After giving Rogers a vague smile, she approached Dr. Kade.

"Mind if I visit with the patient?"

He paid her as much attention as he had Rogers. At least it wasn't personal. "You know the protocol."

Taking that as a yes, she stepped up to the glass.

Forgetting his lack of clothing, he stood and stepped closer to the transparent boundary. "Nia, what's going on?"

"Honestly, I don't know, Steve." Her tone was friendly, but smacked of a well-practiced bedside manner.

"Is it the rabies?"

She shrugged. "If it is, there's no cause for concern." As she spoke, her eyes darted along his muscular body. It wasn't sexual— more the way a doctor would give a visual examination. "Even if a stray bit of saliva entered an open wound, you've no symptoms. A course of immunoglobulin would…"

She stopped and stared at him, puzzled.

"What?"

"It's just… You don't have any scars. You've been in *countless* battles, and you don't have any scars."

"That's not exactly true. I do have one." He twisted and slightly lowered the elastic band on his underwear, revealing a stiff, whitish mesh on his hip about the size of a silver dollar. His expression grew grim as he explained the source.

"It happened during the war. I was holding onto the end of a drone-plane when it exploded. A flaming piece of the engine hit me. Apparently, I held onto it all the way down."

She pressed her hand to the glass near it. "But that's all?"

"I'm resilient, but I'm not Wolverine—or, thank heavens, Deadpool. I heal at a normal rate, but my body tends to do it without scarring. Plus, S.H.I.E.L.D. hires the best doctors." He nodded toward Kade. "If not always the friendliest."

She lowered her voice, but spoke with unconcealed admiration. "Dr. Kade was an intern in Germany in 1967, during the Marburg outbreak. Marburg is a slightly kinder cousin of Ebola, and this was the first we'd seen of such a thing. For a few days, he and the staff were convinced the world was about to end, but he selflessly treated the victims and became infected. Most survivors lost *all* their hair, but the effects weren't just cosmetic: It also damaged his nervous system. Since then he's spent his life going from hot zone to hot zone. Just last year he singlehandedly prevented an Ebola outbreak in Manfi, a West African village. As far as I'm concerned, the lack of social skills is his business. His work is impeccable, his devotion…obsessive."

Rogers held up the laptop. "Kind of got that from his taste in film. Speaking of which, all this waiting's got me thinking. If not drinks, maybe we could catch a movie? I prefer action films, but in your case, I might be willing to take in a comedy."

"You're asking me *now*?" She chuckled and lowered her head. "Seriously?"

"Well, no...a comedy."

She leaned against the wall, holding her index finger against the glass. "Finding a time we're both free—that might be an adventure in itself."

"Is that a yes or a..."

The lab door opened again. S.H.I.E.L.D. Director Nick Fury stormed in with his usual lack of ceremony. Even in his fitted one-piece field suit, the veteran with an eyepatch and a face full of stubble managed to look grizzly.

"Dr. Kade, I appreciate you crossing all your t's, but my eyes are getting crossed." His low, gruff voice made it sound like he was growling. "It's time to tell my country's greatest hero why he's still stuck in that fish tank."

Rogers briefly raised his hand to meet Nia's finger. "Looks like my wait is over. We'll pick this up again later."

"I look forward to it."

Meanwhile, despite the director's request, Kade was still making notes. Rogers didn't know whether to feel sorry for him, or impressed.

"It wouldn't be appropriate. I'm still trying to confirm..."

Fury put his callused thumb and forefinger on the doctor's PDA and tugged it away.

"I hate repeating myself. Tell the man why he's still here."

If Kade wanted to object, something about the glare of the director's single eye stopped him. "Very well."

He straightened his lab coat, and with Fury close behind him, stepped up to the isolation chamber. Even then he hesitated, exhaling and looking around as if trying to find the right words.

"Do I have rabies?" Rogers offered.

"No. You don't have rabies. It's nothing from the bomb."

"What, then?"

Fury's intent stare seemed to physically push Kade. "That's what I've been trying to figure out. I wish I could take credit for seeing what all those who've examined you previously did not, but this new scanner is 800 times more powerful than a nuclear magnetic resonance spectrometer. That's why I was the first to detect this."

Before Rogers could ask, *detect what?* Kade said, "You have a virus."

When he went silent again, Fury prodded him. "Your report said he's had it a while now?"

"Decades. The indications are that he contracted it while frozen in the ice. It may have passed into him from the water or some other frozen organism."

Rogers shook his head. "I don't know that much about viruses. How is that possible?"

The more abstract question seemed to lessen Kade's discomfort. "A viroid's crystal structure allows it to survive nearly any conditions, even the void of space. A few months ago, an ancient virus was found in the Siberian permafrost and dated to at least 30,000 years ago. The moment it thawed, it became infectious. If they didn't occupy a gray area between living and non-living, I'd say they're potentially immortal. It's fascinating to—"

Fury cut him off. "Try to stay on subject—the subject being Cap."

Kade again hesitated, searching for the right words.

Nia spoke up, trying to prompt him. "We live with billions of viruses. Most aren't dangerous. If he's been asymptomatic for so many years, is there any reason to think this one is?"

"There is—a very good reason, in fact—but I didn't want to discuss it before I was certain. The new scanner provided such a detailed image, I was able to use the mainframe here to create a virtual model showing how the virus would behave in a normal human body not buttressed by the Super-Soldier serum." His face grew grim. "Based on my preliminary analysis, we're looking at an EL pathogen."

Nia went slack-jawed. Rogers looked at the two doctors. "Meaning?"

She tried to answer, but couldn't quite finished the sentence. "Extinction level. Able to wipe out..."

Kade finished for her. "The species."

Fury bristled. "That's what the report said, but I still don't get this. He's been walking around with this virus all this time, breathing and bleeding all over the place. Even if he's immune, why hasn't he infected anyone?"

"I've been trying to figure that out. I have a video that may help explain the mechanics, if you'll..." Feebly, he gestured at the PDA in Fury's pocket.

Fury snapped it out and handed it over.

Kade brought up an animation—a bumpy sphere floating in blackness. "This is a single viroid, a simple icosahedral structure." As the angle grew closer, what looked like a solid surface was revealed as a series of spikes. "Those spikes are made of proteins that can adhere to specific receptors on the... Uh... Well, perhaps it might be easier to think of them as skeleton keys—thousands of skeleton keys. When the viroid hits the wall of a healthy cell, it uses its keys to try to get in. If one fits, the viroid not only enters—it's carried right up to the nucleus, where it bursts, releasing its genetic code. The nucleus picks up the pattern, helplessly copying it over and over until the cell explodes. One viroid enters, millions come out. In a human body with a hundred trillion cells, a few million is a drop in the bucket. The immune system can kill most viruses—or we can teach it to, with vaccines. As long as it destroys the viroids faster than they're created, there's no problem. If it can't, the viroids spread until the host becomes symptomatic."

The animation stopped. "That's essentially what we know about how a virus spreads. In this your case, though, the virus has plenty of keys—five times the usual number—but it's not using any of them."

The others looked up from the screen as Kade shook his head. "In all honesty, I have no idea why humanity is still here."

But kill them all and what does it matter?

THE SKYLIGHTS in the crumbling castle's angled ceiling only brought the gloom of an overcast day into the makeshift exam room. Purchasing it anonymously, Johann Schmidt had the interior discreetly, but completely, renovated. The arched windows projected an illusion of broken glass, empty halls, and flaking plaster. Other than stories about hall-wandering ghosts and heart-shaped ponds that filled with blood during full moons, the sparse locals believed it abandoned. In reality, gray-uniformed figures patrolled the modern, highly secure sanctuary.

"A body such as mine simply shouldn't be feeling under the weather, should it?" Johann Schmidt asked. The feeling of not being in control was beginning to wear on the *Roter Totenkopf*—or in the base English, Red Skull.

"A few more minutes, *mein Herr*. I have not finished the analysis. It would be a disservice to us both to supply less than the most accurate information."

Was that it? Or was the doctor hesitating to give him bad news? Schmidt had known the brilliant geneticist Arnim Zola for decades, but it'd become difficult to tell what he was thinking ever since he'd adopted that android body. The expression on its virtual face was more a decision than a reflex, lacking what poker players and interrogators would call a "tell."

The placement of that projected face in the center of Zola's chest didn't help. It made the geneticist look like a Blemmyes, one of the mythical beings once believed to inhabit remote parts of the world. Adolf Hitler, the man they'd both served so long ago, would have taken this choice as a mystic sign affirming the Eternal Reich's connection to the antediluvian world. Zola simply considered it a wiser spot than dangling as an extremity that might easily be lopped off.

Correcting evolution, he once called it. *You can't lose your head if you don't have one.*

A rare joke, if it had been. That was as hard to judge as his current emotional state. His reticence was increasingly frustrating—and suspicious.

Usually, Zola's tongue was looser during his visits to Roscoe, New York. The Swiss-medieval style of the building was a pleasant reminder of the doctor's homeland. Erected in 1921, the design was intended to do the same for the architect's wife, but she'd been committed to a sanitarium before its completion.

It was a perfect place to relax, to plan, to talk. But since the beginning of the exam, Zola's words had been few and far between. He'd seen other bearers of bad news die at the Skull's hands. Was he concerned he might join them?

Schmidt considered reassuring him he was far too valuable to kill, but there was no pleasure in that. Better to let him wonder. Better to keep him alert.

If Zola was worried for himself. There was another, odd, possibility: He might be afraid for the Skull.

The thought angered him. "*Schnell.* Tell me already. What has your examination uncov—?"

Schmidt doubled over, unable to complete his question. A sudden, sickly sweat poured from the red skin that had earned him his nickname, running down his neck to his shoulders. Previously, the icy feeling that made him request the checkup was no more than the sting of a cold needle. Now it sprouted long-fingered branches that cupped the base of his brain.

His eyesight blurred. He shook. One knee buckled; he thought he would fall.

Perhaps forgetting that his inhuman body was no longer subject to infection, the android hesitated before moving toward him to help. Infuriated by his lack of control, Schmidt found the strength to wave him away. Unsure where to direct his anger, he tried to stand. Staggering from the exam table, he supported himself against the bank of monitors that tracked not only the halls, but also his many covert economic and political activities around the world.

They tilted left, then right.

"What's happening to me?" The weakness in his own voice surprised and revolted him.

Finally, Zola answered. "At first, I thought it was some new reaction from your body. As we know, it is an unusual body—and not exactly yours."

At the end of World War II, an experimental gas had placed the Skull in suspended animation, prolonging his life. Years later, when its effects were reversed, it looked to the world as if Johann Schmidt had succumbed to old age. But it was only his body that withered to dust. After all, what is a man, truly, but willful patterns imposed on dull matter? Before the wizened shell could suck its last rattling breath, the brilliant Zola managed to transfer those willful patterns into a new host: a clone grown from the stolen DNA of his nemesis, Captain America.

"*Ja. His* body. Have I ever told you how repugnant I find that?"

As he leaned against the control panel for support, the pain receded. Feeling Zola still at his back, Schmidt again waved him away. Taking a few respectful steps back, the android managed something akin to a shrug.

"Often. I should think his resemblance to the blond, blue-eyed Aryan ideal would have pleased you. But in any case, it is not the cloned body that is causing your symptoms."

Schmidt had to admit it had been reliably powerful until now. Even an encounter with the Dust of Death hadn't killed him. It did, however, leave his visage a desiccated set of bones barely covered by taut, scarlet skin. His form still resembled the Super-Soldier, but his face became the mask he had previously worn for decades—leaving him neither blond nor blue-eyed.

"Your sense of humor is improving, but Rogers was an asthmatic weakling, puny as the *Untermensch* the *Führer* eliminated in the camps. His own country rejected him until—" Another pang made him wince. "If it is not this *verdammt* body, what is it?"

"You have a virus—a very unusual virus. The equipment here is limited, but from what I can tell, instead of traveling through your bloodstream, it's binding to your nerve endings—similar to the manner in which rabies progresses. Could you have come in contact with the strain you provided to the Somali pirates?"

The glow of the monitors hurt the Skull's eyes, so he turned toward his companion. "I haven't left this base in months, before the Somali operation was even planned. The purchases and deliveries were made through intermediaries, all of whom were eliminated once their tasks were complete."

"And you paid in full, in advance? Any person who traffics in such diseases should be given no reason to exact revenge."

Schmidt eyed him. "Do you take me for a fool? Of course he was paid, and paid well. Can you tell me what you *do* know?"

"That won't prove very satisfying, I'm afraid. The data is contradictory. The virus should be highly communicable—and lethal. With such a short gestation period, I am tempted to call it an extinction-level pathogen."

"A dramatic assessment."

"It is. At the same time, none of your men are symptomatic. Though given my understanding of viruses, I suspect they will be soon."

A shaky Schmidt rubbed his bony chin. It felt dry. At least the sweating had stopped. He looked up at the monitors, at his loyal followers all at their stations. "A simple interaction with a delivery truck could carry it to the outside world, could it not?"

"It could."

"And the authorities would be able to trace it back here."

"They might."

"Then adjustments must be made to counter that possibility. I did not spend months constructing this hideaway to have it so easily revealed."

He flicked a lever, sealing the room. He heard Zola say, "Before you do anything..." but his voice sounded distant, muffled.

The Skull ignored him. He was in control. He flicked another lever, and a light hissing echoed from beyond the door. The air-quality readouts turned red. Moments later, one guard grabbed his throat and fell. Another rushed over to help—but before he could reach the man's side, he dropped, as well.

"*Herr* Skull, you may not be thinking clearly."

Feeding an old fascination, the Skull's eyes moved from image to image, watching his followers gasp and fall. As the bodies twitched, he remained riveted, staring until there was no further movement. Another switch activated the ventilation fans. The readouts turned green as the air quality returned to normal.

"That was...impetuous," Zola said.

His mood improved, the Skull responded, "At least we now know the ventilation system operates as expected." He walked over to the leather chair behind his mahogany desk and sat. "But my apologies. Did you have objections?"

"I see little point in mentioning them now."

Schmidt leaned back, folded his gloved hands in his lap and offered the android a smile. "I insist, Arnim. Please, correct my *impetuousness*."

"My objections are purely strategic. If one of those men brought the virus, you have placed him beyond even my interrogation techniques. If any were infected—and I never said they were—I could have used additional samples from a normal body. Lastly, the corpses will have to be incinerated to ensure the virus is destroyed. If discovery was your main concern, the smoke could also attract attention."

Realizing he was right, Schmidt struggled to keep his voice even. "Perhaps in the future you might stop me *before* I make such amateurish mistakes."

"I tried. But you misinterpret my assessment. I don't consider your actions amateurish. As I said, the virus affects the nervous system, including the brain. Such rash self-indulgence may be a symptom of the disease."

Feeling a twinge, the Skull pressed his fingers to his temples. When he withdrew them, they were again damp with sweat. "Then we mustn't delay. Prepare to transfer my essence, as you call it, to another, less distasteful body as soon as possible. You have the necessary equipment here, *ja*?"

Ja. His old accent seemed to be thickening, as well. Another symptom?

The face on the android's chest frowned. "I fear, *Herr* Skull, that because of the virus's peculiar relationship to the nervous system, that won't be possible."

Summoning his strength, the Skull straightened and managed a confident grin. "This is no time for defeatism, Arnim. Relying on your brilliance, I have survived impossible odds before. We must trust I will do so again. Prepare your equipment."

"Again, you don't understand. To speak of *odds* is inaccurate. Already the virus has become so intertwined with your higher functions that transferring your essence will also transfer the virus. In any form, even binary, it will continue replacing your pattern with its own. Giving you a new body would change nothing."

The grin slightly faded. "Now, now—you have surprised me before."

"But I have yet to surprise myself. And while I appreciate your faith, in this case, unless some miraculous cure is found, you *will* die."

Death only matters to those left behind.

THERE was never any question Captain America would put others above himself. He'd done it so often, so instinctually, that someone lacking his ethic might consider it a psychological condition in need of medication. Even those gathered in the lab who knew him by reputation only, didn't doubt he'd do the same here.

If anything, Steve Rogers thought as he watched from behind the glass, they might take unnecessary risks on his behalf. Nick Fury, for instance, who had known him the longest, had ordered that the hastily convened meeting take place entirely in Rogers' presence—and with his input. The gruff S.H.I.E.L.D. director had a small conference table brought into the lab, forcing the collected department heads to sit in uncomfortably close folding chairs. Fury claimed he'd do the same for any agent, or civilian, in similar cir-cumstances, but clearly it had more than a little to do with the specific person involved.

Rogers had read, via the laptop, about how fast pathogens could spread, and it gave him pause. The average person touched their own face about a thousand times a day. As he counted the stray scratches, the nose-rubbing, the lip-wiping, the hands passing through hair, Nia picking at a nail, the number seemed low.

The only one who didn't make any such gestures was Kade. If there was even the remotest danger, he was confident the epidemiologist would've objected fiercely. Since discovering the virus, the only kindness Kade'd shown was the clothing he'd placed in the small secure-transfer unit that opened into the sealed chamber. When Rogers offered to return the doctor's laptop the same way, he backed away, suggesting Steve "just keep it, for now."

The white jumpsuit was more apropos to the meeting than his underpants, but Steve felt no less like a lab rat. Fortunately, Fury was doing enough pacing for both of them, marching tiger-like along his end of the table. Before everyone could finish wedging themselves in place, he pointed at the wall-projected agenda.

"Okay, kiddies, time for this week's imminent threat to humanity. Item one, potential-exposure group, which I gotta figure means *everyone*, right? Dawson?"

Pinned in place, the fair-haired man, a relative newcomer to S.H.I.E.L.D.'s medical staff, tried not to shift as he spoke. "It would be impossible to list everyone Patient Zero...uh, Captain Rogers, has been in contact with the last few decades, but we have to start somewhere. The Helicarrier will remain under quarantine until everyone onboard has been cleared: no arrivals, and no departures. Eighteen percent of personnel have already been through the new scanner. Any agent or staff here who worked with him in any capacity in the last six months has been prioritized. That processing rate will double once the backup scanner is up and running, and we're en route to pick up a third via unmanned drone at a Stark

Industries complex in Naples. Even without it, a conservative estimate gives us complete coverage of all 1,827 crew and guests within 34 hours."

Fury blasted some air through his nose. "Don't bury the lead. You find anything?"

Dawson shook his head. "No. Based on the model Dr. Kade provided, a specific plus-strand RNA polygon with an atypical protein coat, we've had no further viroid identifications."

"Meaning it hasn't spread. Good."

Kade cleared his throat. "As far as we know."

Fury turned his good eye toward Kade. "We've all read your new report, doc. I even had the big words translated into English for me. This is my staff's opportunity to fill in any blanks. So I'd like to hear from them first, if you don't mind."

Kade looked down.

Fury continued. "Item two, theories. According to our esteemed guest, Cap's been infected at *least* since he was on ice. If it was *during*, that likely means contact occurred through natural causes. What have we got on that end, Milo?"

A veteran of the U.S. Army Medical Research Institute of Infectious Diseases, Janet Milo had been with S.H.I.E.L.D. medical for seven years. She didn't have to check her notes. "If it's reoviridae, it could use practically anything as a host—humans, animals, even plants or fungi. Captain Rogers might have contracted it through some prehistoric algae that'd been frozen for millennia..."

Listening quietly from the edge of the chamber bed, Rogers could contribute almost nothing. There were no combat decisions to make, no attack plans to formulate. At the same time, sitting by while others debated his fate felt familiar. He reached for the memory, but it remained at arm's length.

When Milo finished, Kade looked as if he wanted to speak again. Fury pointedly moved on. "If he was infected *before* being frozen, that opens up the possibility it was intentional, which brings us to Agent Barca."

A lean, curly haired man with a goatee answered. "It could be a stealth virus, an engineered strain. Something like that could remain dormant for decades until it was activated by a predetermined stimuli, like a bomb waiting for a signal from a cellphone."

Fury grimaced. "Yeah, but who was weaponizing viruses in World War II?"

Barca shrugged. "Weaponized viruses are nothing new, Colonel. In 1500 B.C., the Hittites sent plague victims into enemy lands. This specific sort of thing is beyond any technology we're aware of—but in terms of possibilities, Arnim Zola experimented with genetic engineering in the 1940s. He, or some unknown, may have made the necessary breakthroughs."

Rogers stiffened at the name. It was a lead, at least something to think about—until Fury voiced the obvious objection.

"If some evil genius went through all the trouble of setting up Cap as the ultimate time bomb, wouldn't they have asked for ransom by now? Sixty years is a long time to save something this big for a rainy day."

Barca had already thought that through. "If we assume they're still around. Remember, Captain Rogers was believed dead for decades. The perpetrator may have died of old age in the meantime. The problem may already be solved."

Kade half-rose from his seat. "Those are a lot of 'ifs.'"

Fury let a beat pass. "I've been working this end of the desk a real long time, and 'a lot of ifs' is all I've ever had. The fact is, this thing hasn't spread for years. The only real difference between yesterday and today is that now we know about it. Maybe his immune system keeps it in check. Hell, maybe it's a freakin' *magical* virus. But given how you're so eager to talk out of turn, let me ask you: Once we've completed our due diligence here, is there any solid reason we shouldn't let him out of that cage?"

As if watching a slow-motion tennis match, Rogers and the tight-packed crowd shifted their gaze back to Kade. The two speakers were a study in contrasts. Muscled Fury, a man with extreme faith in his instincts, waited for a response. Kade—physically slight, living far more in his own head than his damaged body—answered matter-of-factly.

"Technically, because I won't permit it."

All eyes snapped toward Fury. "You...what? Last I heard, I'm the one giving orders here."

Kade strummed his fingers on the tabletop. "Well, no. You, uh, should have been notified by now."

As if on cue, devices beeped across the table. Rogers' borrowed laptop—now connected to the network—displayed an official-looking notice. As he scanned it, Kade explained.

"I've contacted the CDC. Under international protocol, in these circumstances, their mandate exceeds S.H.I.E.L.D.'s. I've been given control over any decisions regarding the containment of this virus."

Fury glanced up from reading; his visible eye flared. "Son of a..."

Kade blinked. "I don't mean to step on anyone's toes."

"You've got a funny way of showing it!"

"I appreciate your confusion and your ignorance..."

"My...what?" The director looked as if he might lunge across the table. A few agents tensed, prepared to hold him back.

Kade showed no sign of fear or remorse. "...but the situation is too extreme. I can't rely on a layman to understand the extent of the danger, especially given the understandable esteem Captain Rogers enjoys among your people. Your thinking is obviously muddied by your loyalty. Mine isn't. I agreed to this meeting because the isolation chamber is secure, but he'll remain there until I say otherwise."

Fury leaned forward in a way that didn't relax those who knew him. "Protecting humanity from extinction is what S.H.I.E.L.D. does. If you think some—"

"Before you continue, let me give you an example of how you're not thinking clearly. You just said that the only difference between yesterday and today is that now we know about this virus. What if it wasn't a virus? What if we'd discovered an asteroid heading toward the Earth?"

"I'll give you an asteroid...."

Fury came forward, not stopping until Dawson and Milo moved to grab him. It was time for the lab rat to intervene.

Rogers knocked on the glass—hard, but not too hard—to get their attention. "Fury...Nick, let the man talk, then take it from there."

Fury threw up his hands and sat back down. "Like I have a choice?"

The room breathed a collected sigh of relief. Even Kade, perhaps finally realizing his bedside manner might need to be improved, took a moment to gather his thoughts. The doctor's abrupt rise to power seemed appropriate enough to Rogers, but it still increased his disquiet. Why?

He'd been imprisoned, trapped, seemingly helpless many times, but this was uncomfortably familiar. Was it because the nuances were beyond his expertise? Was it because he was afraid?

Of course he was afraid. He'd never lacked fear, as some might think. He wanted to live, to thrive, to enjoy the pleasures that the world had to offer. But a long time ago, he'd decided that desire would never be fulfilled at someone else's expense. That choice allowed him to push aside his fear. Reaffirmed again and again, in countless ways over countless battles, it had become a matter of routine.

As if finishing a long drink of water, Kade swallowed, straightened, and cleared his throat. "Saving humanity is also what I do, but my expertise doesn't involve criminal masterminds or non-terrestrial threats. I wouldn't dream of second-guessing S.H.I.E.L.D. under any of those circumstances. But my work does involve this *specific* type of threat, and I know that if we're not extremely cautious, we could be staring at a Black Swan event—something utterly unexpected in human history, until it occurs."

Fury bristled. "I *know* what it means. We've had six Black Swans in the last five years. But like I said, Steve's been out there, breathing, bleeding, and saving asses for longer than that. If *anyone* had been infected in all that time, we'd have noticed, don't you think?"

"That's the point. By the time we see an infection, it will be too late. You appreciate testosterone, so I'll try to put it in familiar terms. Picture a cocked gun aimed directly at our species, rigged with a tripwire. The world's leading expert is telling you the wire *has* been tripped. The gun should have gone off, but it hasn't. We can't just *hope* it stays that way. We either have to confirm that it *can't* go off, or figure out some way to unload the gun." He paused, then added, "By which I mean a vaccine, or a cure."

Fury glowered. "I know how analogies work, too. And I'm a real whiz at ciphering. I get your point, but answer me—" Once again, devices across the room began to beep. "Oh, for the love of... Put those things in movie mode!"

Nia turned toward Fury. "I apologize for the interruption, Colonel. I didn't realize how quickly they'd respond."

Kade looked at his PDA and frowned. "Another CDC notice. Apparently, my authority isn't to be quite as complete as I announced. Any actions I take must also be approved by Dr. N'Tomo." He looked at her.

She shrugged. "I didn't feel it appropriate for one person to make these calls, especially with another qualified expert present."

"I'll welcome your input."

Uncertain how he should react to the news, Fury twisted his lips. "Maybe I should go for a stroll along the boulevard, and you two can text me if I'm needed."

Ignoring him the way a parent might ignore a petulant child, Kade addressed Nia. "You realize we can't keep Captain Rogers in that quarantine chamber indefinitely."

Fury brightened. "So we do agree on *something*?"

Nia shook her head. "No, I believe Dr. Kade is referring to the fact that since this viroid's never been detected before, it's never been contained before. Therefore we can't be certain any existing procedures will work. With the stakes so extreme, we should think in extreme terms."

Kade nodded. "Exactly."

The colonel's upper lip curled. "Oh, so you think we should just whack him?"

Kade refused to react to the sarcasm. "If he were an animal and it was safe to grow the virus in a culture, that's precisely what I'd suggest. In this case, accurate as the computer modeling might be, destruction of the only living host would make it impossible to verify the efficacy of a potential treatment."

Around the table, faces dropped and eyes widened. When Kade noticed, he added, "And...of course, he has a right to survive."

Though his addendum did little to alter their expressions, he went on. "I do have another plan, one that Dr. N'Tomo will now apparently have to approve."

The tightly packed space making movement difficult, he slowly crossed the lab and activated a projector. A blueprint appeared next to Fury's bulleted list. "Viruses replicate based on the speed of the host's metabolism. The best way to ensure containment would be to slow that metabolism by placing the patient in this."

Fury's mouth dropped open. "That's a cryo-cylinder! Are you telling me you want to take a guy who's already spent 60 years on ice and freeze him again?"

Kade nodded. "Yes. Wasn't that clear? Not permanently, but for...a while. Given the modeling enabled by the new scanner, and factoring in the current rate of technological advances, a treatment plan should be obtainable within twenty years. Forty years would be an outside estimate."

Rogers felt sucker-punched. *Forty years. I'll wake up in a completely different world. Everyone I know will either be gone or nearing the end of their time. Again.*

Apparently unable to believe what he was hearing, Fury looked to Nia, his tone oddly pleading. "Please, tell me he's crazy."

Her grim expression told them all what she would say. "I'd very much like to disagree with Dr. Kade, but I can't. The potential threat based on the computer models is staggering. The precaution... makes sense."

As she spoke, it finally dawned on Rogers why the scene felt so familiar.

He *had* been here before, at the very beginning: a lab rat, but a willing one, so very, very eager to be given the chance—just the *chance*—to serve a greater cause. The fact that the combination of Dr. Erskine's Super-Soldier serum and the vita-rays could kill him hadn't really occurred to him until the moment the needles pierced his skin.

Even then, it was worth it.

And wasn't this the same situation?

His heart ached at the thought of another long sleep. But trusting Nia, even trusting Kade in his way, made it easier. He rapped on the glass again and gave them all his most sincere smile.

"If that's how it has to be, let's do it."

If they're all gone, what's left to care? The sky? The planet?
The stars? No.

HAVING methodically incinerated the corpses and disposed of the ashes, Arnim Zola returned to the castle's upper level. The lights were off in the main room, the control center quietly lit by the fireplace and monitor glow. Schmidt stood behind his desk bathed partly in reddish yellow, partly in electronic blue. A wooden crate was open before him. In it lay five antique German crystal steins packed in straw. His visible hand cupped a sixth stein, half-filled with Pilsner.

He raised it to greet the android.

"I like this mix of old and new. It reminds me...of myself." He took a sip and exhaled a raspy sigh. "I'd like to show you something, doctor."

With an odd, bemused expression, Schmidt raised his other arm and held out a clenched fist. Turning it over beneath his gaze, he regarded the appendage as if it were a curio he'd picked up in the same antique store as the steins.

"My own hand, and I can't move it at all. A new symptom?"

Zola shook his digital head. "Of the virus? No. Too soon."

"What, then?"

"Given my understanding of your psychology, I suspect you are simply experiencing extreme anger regarding your fate and somatizing that feeling."

Schmidt nodded, considering the idea. "Anger. Hm."

A shifting log popped in the fireplace. For a moment, all was silent. Then, his scarlet face twisting, the Skull slammed his frozen fist onto the desk. With a crack like thunder, a dark line snaked along the mahogany surface. The steins rattled in their straw.

When he raised his arm, he found he could flex his fingers again. For him, the slight curl at the edges of his rows of bared teeth was an expression of pleasure. For others, it was the stuff of nightmares. "Ah. I suspect you were correct."

"I can give you an antidepressant."

The Skull was genuinely curious. "Why?"

"Comfort? Increased clarity?" Zola offered. "There is no shame in it. Anxiety is not unusual under the circumstances."

"Anxiety? You mean fear, not anger, then?"

"If you prefer. The terms at least overlap. Sensing a threat, the body seeks fight or flight."

One moment, Schmidt seemed to be thinking about it. The next, he grabbed one of the empty steins and hurled it against the mantle. The hard crystal exploded, briefly filling the air with tiny reflections of yellow, red, and blue. After scanning the broken pieces, he turned back to his companion.

"You disappoint me. Rage is not fear. That's like comparing a burning star to mud. Fear is weakness. Rage is the will growing taut, preparing to act." His eyes narrowed. "Do you have any idea what rare ecstasies I'd have been denied without my rage? Never to experience, for instance, the joy of strangling the woman I loved for daring to reject me? No, Zola, anger does not require sedation. It demands respect."

"I see your point…" The android turned slightly as another beer stein flew across the small space between the Skull and the fireplace. "…as did the object of your affections. I did not mean to suggest your righteous fury should be equated with weakness. At the same time, it's natural to dread one's mortality, is it not?"

Schmidt scoffed. "Since when do you and I care for nature?" He held out the stein from which he still drank, first to the flames, then to the monitors. "There's nature for you. Fire held in place by fieldstone, electric current made obedient to the resistance of a silicon chip. Why bow to something that exists only to be tamed?" He picked up a fourth stein and threw it. "And rage? Without its power to focus the will, life becomes as pointless as these broken bits of crystal scattered on the floor."

"May I ask what your rage demands of you now?"

His eyes widened. "Survival, of course. It demands survival."

Zola looked at the Skull, then the shattered crystals, then back at the Skull. "I may have misspoke when I said your clenched hand was not caused by the virus. The disease can…enhance your mood."

"Then this virus has benefits." He drained the only remaining stein of his contents. "I have not lived so long just to die, and most certainly not at the hands of nature."

"As I've already explained, I will do what I can, but we all have limits."

"Great as your reach may be, Zola, your limits and mine are not the same."

When he threw the last stein, it shattered like the others. Unlike them, its base was not empty. What looked like a small brass-colored tuning fork glittered among the shards.

"Ah, the thing we seek is always found in the last place we look, *ja*?" Absently massaging one hand with the other, Schmidt cleared the crystal bits from the object with the toe of his boot. "At least I finished my beer."

"You have some specific plan?"

"Of course. Planning is what I do. From the day I fled the orphanage, to my rise in Nazi Germany, to this very moment, I've been planning." He bent to pick up the object. When he held it out toward Zola, the ghastly smile returned. "It's not as if some other hobby would suffice."

The android approached for a closer look. The Skull obliged, bringing it into the firelight and turning over the shapes of its three prongs in his hand: circle, square, and triangle. There were electronics visible in the cylindrical handle—but crude, as if hand-made—with thin filaments crossing the three prongs.

"Wonderfully intricate, is it not? A mesh of the pragmatic and the beautiful, made years before Werner Jacobi took credit for inventing the integrated circuit." He raised an eyebrow at the android. "Do you recognize it, Arnim? Speak plainly. I will not be angry."

"From its appearance, it was part of the Reich's secret weapons program. I was intimately familiar with all those projects. My memory of them is photographic, enhanced by my form. Therefore I *should* know what it is, but..." Zola's avatar made a rare frown. "...

this is not something I've ever seen."

The answer satisfied any suspicions the Skull had. "It is called the Sonikey, and you were not meant to recognize it. Nor was I. Had we not lost so many secrets to treacherous spies and the cretins of the All-Winners Squad, any one of our technological break-throughs would have turned the course of the war. So, for this project, *der Führer* trusted no one. Even the designers and builders were executed upon the project's completion."

"In that case, I suppose I should be thankful I don't recognize it."

"He even had this key surgically implanted in his body," Schmidt said with a chuckle, "which made retrieving it...interesting."

Zola turned his scanners on the device. "It appears to be a crude version of the soni-crystal, the device used to awaken *der Schläfer*, the Sleepers. An earlier effort at the same goal?"

The Skull regarded the object with a sort of grudging fascina-tion. "Close, but not entirely correct. The Sleepers were the ultimate expression of Hitler's scorched-earth policy. They were built to de-stroy the world if he could not conquer it. One humanoid, one winged, one an enormous bomb—the first three were to join to-gether, dig their way close to the Earth's core, and detonate. The fourth was a living volcano, meant to speed the planet's geologic destruction. The fifth, an unstoppable tank intended to overwhelm any who tried to stop the others. Had they been used that way, they might have fulfilled their purpose."

The recitation kept them both entranced, conjuring images of a giant's riveted feet; of vast metallic wings that blocked out the sun, darkening the sky; and the bomb that prefigured, yet exceeded, the first nuclear weapons.

Only Schmidt's loud *tsk* brought them back into the room. "But instead I tried to use them piecemeal for my own plans. After all, one needs the world intact in order to conquer it."

Seeing no need to mention the blur of red, white, and blue that had prevailed against the enormous machines, he fell silent.

Zola's question, by dint of his nature, was pragmatic. "If you knew there were more Sleepers, why keep them hidden? There were countless times you could have used such power."

Resentment flashed in Schmidt's eyes. "Because their very existence is an insult. They were built based on the notion that I might fail to destroy Captain America. At the time, Hitler was unable to imagine his own defeat, but he did consider the possibility he might be driven into hiding. These, the very first Sleepers, were intended to seek out democracy's most powerful propaganda symbol, analyze his weaknesses, and assemble into a fearsome battle suit designed solely to obliterate him. And would Hitler give that honor to me, his right hand? No. He intended to wear it himself. Captain America's death at his hands would show the world the Reich had risen again." He closed his fingers around the object and squeezed until it was lost from sight. "But destroying Rogers was *my* mission, you see. And I have no idea where the pieces were hidden, or even what they look like!"

For a moment, Schmidt worried his hand had seized again. With some effort, he opened his fist and stared at what it held. "Wounded pride may have blinded me to other opportunities, yet I still have the Sonikey today as a result."

The Skull squinted at a dried fleck on its edge. "A bit of dried intestine, I believe. Useful for your experiments?"

"No, thank you. I have plenty of those DNA samples. I was thinking that splicing them with the genes of a house cat might make for an interesting, if obstinate, pet. But let me say I admire your choice to die in battle with your greatest foe."

"Didn't you hear me? I do not plan to die at all. I admit not knowing all the project details—the power source is particularly mysterious—but I do know the battle suit was designed to keep its occupant alive under the most extreme circumstances imaginable. Apparently our former leader was concerned that when the time came he might be quite old, even ill."

Zola remained dubious. "The Nazi researchers could imagine quite a few human extremes, given the experiments they conducted in the camps, but I'm afraid even they could not stop this virus."

"Careful, doctor. Your pragmatism begins to border on pessimism. I don't imagine the Sleepers will provide a cure—just a way to outlive your prognosis. If the suit keeps me alive an extra month, there may be a way to extend that even further. Do you think you could find a cure in a year?"

"I don't know."

Perhaps Schmidt should have expected the robotically neutral answer. Instead, he found himself wondering how much an android interested in "correcting" evolution would genuinely care if he, or all humanity for that matter, perished.

But he had to trust *someone*.

"Now, now." Schmidt nodded again toward the pile of broken crystal. "That glass was half full, why not another?"

"Very well. If I don't know that I will fail, it's possible I will succeed."

Schmidt pressed a button on the base of the Sonikey. Low lights danced along its surface—thin lines traveling an intricate copper path, growing thicker and stronger as they moved faster and faster.

The Red Skull sneered. "And if nothing else, at least I will destroy Rogers."

History doesn't exist without someone reading it.

VACATIONING in Paris to celebrate her new linguistics degree, Pennsylvania-born Sabine Fertig had already taken her photo with the large metal and glass *Pyramide du Louvre* at the main entrance to the famous museum. Now she was in the nearby mall, hoping to do the same with *La Pyramide Inversée*, a smaller, upside-down version that acted as a magnificent skylight.

Like millions of others, she'd read the famous 2003 novel in which the little solid pyramid beneath the skylight was secretly the tip of a full-size, buried tomb containing the remains of Mary Magdalene. But that was just a book. Having seen videos of its installation, she knew the stone shape was as it appeared: just three feet tall.

She still wanted a photo, though.

Unable to find an obliging shopper, she was holding her new digital camera out in front of herself and her six-month-old daughter, Irma, when something tiny landed in her eye.

After blinking it out, she looked up, thinking it had fallen from the skylight. When another small object hit her cheek, she pushed Irma and her stroller to a safe distance before looking again.

The sunlight streaming through the faceted glass was bright enough to illuminate a few specks of floating dust, but nothing seemed loose or falling. Chalking up her concern to motherly paranoia, Sabine was about to leave—then rubbed her cheek.

Whatever hit her was still on her skin. Afraid it might be glass, she gingerly plucked it off. Curious, she rubbed it between her thumb and forefinger. It felt like rough stone or concrete. Looking back at the small pyramid on the floor, she noticed a tiny crack along one of its faces.

She pushed the stroller closer. As she did, something too small to make out clearly popped out from one end of the crack and arced to the tiled floor, leaving a tiny cloud of particles hanging in the air along its path.

She backed up, but kept watching.

Was it an insect? Maybe, but it was so tiny—smaller than any insect had a right to be. Did they have especially small insects in Paris? Could it just be a piece of stone? Was the little pyramid crumbling?

She searched her new camera for the video setting. If she caught the crack getting bigger, a clip might be worth something. Another pop—not loud enough to turn heads, but louder than the first—made her decide it was more important to put some distance between Irma and whatever was going on.

A stone wall on the opposite side of the space seemed far enough for safety's sake. Once she reached it, Sabine felt she should tell someone. It was a famous landmark, after all, and she had come to Europe to try out her new degree. A mall guard, bobbing on the balls of his feet with his hands clasped behind his back, stood nearby.

Gamely, she walked up with the stroller. When he looked at her, she smiled and gave him her best French:

"Il ya une fissure dans la petite pyramide."

She was pretty sure she'd said, "There's a crack in the little pyramid."

But the guard only seemed puzzled. *"Une fissure?"*

She nodded enthusiastically. *"Oui, une fissure dans la petite pyramide."*

When this didn't clear things up, she added, *"Je pense que ce pourrait être des ânes."*

She'd hoped to say, "I think it might be insects," but worried she'd used the word for *donkeys* instead. Judging from the guard's reaction, she had. If anything, he seemed a little offended.

"La pyramide est la pierre solide. Il ne peut pas simplement se fissurer."

Something about the pyramid being solid stone, unable to crack. Sabine was about to try to show him the darn crack, but Irma started squealing.

The guard smiled and made a baby face. *"Peut-être que votre enfant a besoin de ses couches changé?"*

But it wasn't a soiled-diaper squeal, a sound Sabine knew well. This was more like Irma's cooing when she'd seen giraffes for the first time, at the *Parc Zoologique de Paris* that morning.

The guard bent over the carriage, smiled, and waved, but Irma ignored him.

Sabine realized Irma was staring at the pyramid.

The crack wasn't simply widening—chunks of stone were falling from it.

Sabine was frozen just long enough to see a flat metal triangle, three feet tall, flop out of the little pyramid as if hatching from a stone egg. By the time other shoppers began to notice, she was already pushing Irma and the carriage toward the nearest exit.

The last she saw of the metal triangle, it was unfolding. Still flat, it was making itself larger, one triangle at a time. After that, she didn't bother looking back. She'd done her duty. It was the guard's problem now.

At first she trotted. When she heard the screams and racing steps behind her, she ran, pushing a now-sobbing Irma as quickly as she could.

"It's all right, it's all right," she said to the carriage.

But a booming voice turned Irma's cries into a wail:

"Wo ist Kapitän Amerika?"

Sabine only assumed the voice was coming from the triangles, but she wasn't about to check. The exit still seemed a million miles away when the voice came again:

"Wo ist Kapitän Amerika?"

It was mechanical, crackly, as if recorded a hundred years ago and played back through poorly connected speakers. At least it didn't sound any closer. It spoke German, another language she knew, but the rush to get her child to safety made her mind a muddle.

Who? Why? What?

Scores of fleeing shoppers on either side, she burst through the exit onto the pavilion outside the Louvre. Once in the open air, it came to her.

Where.

It was saying, over and over: "WHERE IS CAPTAIN AMERICA?"

EVEN before Nia N'Tomo reached the huge cargo bay, she'd been feeling small. Nia had ample experience with the sense of dread nearly all hot-zone workers encounter in the presence of deadly pathogens, but she'd never seen anything remotely like this virus. Though awed by its intricate beauty, she was equally terrified by the implications of its design—and struggling against a growing sense of helplessness.

Contributing to a solution would help, but so far, Dr. Kade had second-guessed her every thought. She'd suggested using the same model he'd used to predict the symptoms to simulate the virus's interactions with known vaccines, only to learn he already had half the Helicarrier's mainframes devoted to the task. There was some comfort in believing a potential "hit" could happen any time, but all the variables made it a roulette game with nearly infinite odds.

There had to be some other path. But like S.H.I.E.L.D., the immune system could only respond to threats it was able to recognize. The T and B lymphocytes that kept viroids from replicating, even tagged them for destruction, relied on known patterns. A vaccine could "teach" the body to destroy a new virus—but something unfamiliar, causing no symptoms, was essentially invisible.

She had left the lab to help Dr. Dawson supervise the arrival of the third scanner. Updating it with the latest viroid model would enable faster detection *and* give her time to follow the flow of her own instincts.

After all, Kade was brilliant, not omniscient. Not that the mainstream press would have you believe otherwise. Hoping to ease their collaboration by being more knowledgeable about his work, Nia briefly looked him up. Scores of news hubs listed his accomplishments, especially in Manfi, but even the few medical sites she had time to check failed to turn up any details that might help her get a better handle on his style.

With the Helicarrier still under quarantine, the delivery from Stark Industries Napoli was made by a drone hover-flier. Watching the pilotless vehicle swoop into its assigned landing spot so effortlessly reminded her how much humanity could achieve. That helped. And though it wasn't a high bar to reach, Dr. Dawson proved far more genial than Kade.

But while the large crate was being loaded on a pallet, the cargo bay erupted with flashing red lights. As klaxons brayed, N'Tomo instinctively grabbed a handrail. Just in time, too. The floor tilted under their feet, and she found herself steadying Dr. Dawson to keep him from falling.

"Are we under attack?" she asked him. "Have we been hit?"

After regaining his balance, he pushed his glasses back up the bridge of his nose and focused on what she thought was a sleek wristwatch—but along with the time, it projected a wealth of real-time data along the white sleeve of his lab coat.

"No, it's a priority-one course change," he said with some relief. "We're responding to an alert in Paris. ETA is about an hour."

An hour? Paris was at least 4,000 kilometers away. How fast could the Helicarrier move?

Before she could ask, Fury's voice was in her ear. "Dr. N'Tomo, you're needed in Lab 247 stat. I gotta clear some agents for field work, and your colleague's giving me a heaping ton of—"

A loud beeping drowned him out. Once the carrier steadied, she headed for the nearest corridor, but hesitated at the sight of the bustling crew.

Dawson called after her. "Do you need help?"

"I'll find it, thanks."

The hurried crew racing to their stations didn't slow her down—she already knew a shortcut. She opened the lab door to find an unsurprising argument in progress: the gaunt Kade holding steady against a freely reddening Col. Fury. Steve Rogers, meanwhile, politely sat in his isolation chamber looking unsure whether to be concerned or amused.

"It would be advisable to allow the local authorities to handle this!"

Fury stepped closer, intentionally invading Kade's personal space. "I keep tellin' you they don't have the training or the equipment to handle a freakin' giant killer robot!" Kade's lack of reaction only made him angrier. "Which of the three words don't you get? Giant, killer, or robot?"

Whatever the threat in Paris actually was, Nia was pleased to think she had an easy compromise. "Why not just use the field agents we've already cleared?"

Kade gritted his teeth. Fury beamed. "THANK you! That's all I've been asking."

Realizing she'd accidentally sided against the world's best epidemiologist, Nia tried to mitigate her tone.

"Which is not to say I don't appreciate the need for caution—"

Fury didn't give her a chance to finish. "But you don't agree."

She thought a moment. The scanner that cleared the agents was the same one that had identified the virus in the first place. If they couldn't trust the scanner, there was no basis to believe the virus existed at all. It was the right call.

"No. I don't."

Giving her a thumbs up, the colonel headed for the door, barking into his comm. "Tell CDC we've got approval to scramble teams one through four. Jacobs is on point. On my way to monitor from the bridge."

Dr. Kade didn't so much as look at her. He just sighed deeply and stepped pointedly back to his work. She was debating whether to approach him, to better explain, when Steve's voice stopped Fury from leaving.

"Nick, from what I'm seeing on the news, this thing is World War II-era Nazi tech."

"What's on the news?" Nia asked.

Still eyeing Fury, Steve held up the laptop for her to see.

Her French was fluent, but she had to look twice before believing the crawl did in fact say *giant killer robot*. Mouth open, she glanced at the director. "I assumed you were using a metaphor."

Fury hadn't moved from the door. "Nah. When you got a giant killer robot, who needs metaphors?"

The rest of the screen showed a shaky feed from a helicopter above the Louvre. Part of the pavilion was covered by what looked like rubble from a huge bomb blast—only the rubble was animate. The dull metal collection took on a variety of hard geometric shapes—but in between, it seemed fluid, like an amoeba.

Newly agitated, Dr. Kade shook a bony finger at the director. "We shouldn't even be discussing this in front of him! And didn't we agree it would be best if he didn't receive any alerts?"

Fury grimaced. "He hasn't. Not from me or my crew. But I guess we both forgot he can stream CNN in there."

Steve ignored them. "Nick, Nazi tech. So...the Skull?"

"Maybe. You, uh...must be getting sound, too, right?"

"Oh, yeah." Steve raised the volume.

A voice, rendered tinny by the small speakers, floated into the lab: *"Wo ist Kapitän Amerika?"*

Kade threw up his hands in disgust. "Well, this is just perfect, isn't it?"

Rogers gave Fury a meaningful look.

"Okay, Cap, okay. Don't let your head swell. That ain't live—it's just some recording from the good old days. The whole thing is probably just an antique weapon the Nazis forgot about that accidentally activated, like those unexploded bombs we used to find all over London."

"Maybe, but I'd recognize that voice anywhere."

Fury nodded. "Adolf Hitler. Yeah, we've already confirmed that it's him."

"Wo ist Kapitän Amerika?"

Steve was on his feet so suddenly, Nia couldn't help but remember that he was not a normal man. "And you weren't planning to mention that it's asking for me?"

Fury crossed his arms over his chest. "No, I wasn't, and you know damn well why. That thing can knock all it wants, but Captain America can't come out to play."

Seeing the director's determination, Kade receded to the back of the lab, and his work. Steve, however, looked as if he might actually pace.

Nia had seen many patients stuck in isolation for weeks, even months. Construction workers, farmers—anyone accustomed to being on the move had the hardest time with it. And here was Captain America. Disciplined as he was, it had to be terribly challenging for him to remain in that small space.

Doubly so when there was a threat calling him out by name.

She turned to Fury. "Colonel, could Captain Rogers act as an adviser to the ground team?"

He nodded instantly. "I usually call the shots, but hell, yeah. I can have the feeds pumped in here."

Steve's face remained stoic, but Nia saw his shoulders relax a bit. "I'll do what I can."

Kade—listening in and apparently still not recovered from his confrontation with Fury—shook as he started to speak. "I'd rather..."

But he didn't finish. He spun back to his desk. "Never mind. It's a good idea, Dr. N'Tomo. At least no one's trying to send him into combat."

Ignoring him, Fury grinned widely at Steve, forcing him to ask, "What?"

"Never thought of you as an armchair general."

Nia smiled with them until her gaze returned to Kade, hunched over the computers, shifting images of proteins, capsids, and nucleic acids. She respected him incredibly, but instead of expressing her admiration, she'd interfered with his role with the CDC. And now, in minutes, she'd stepped on his toes twice more.

She should speak with him privately, clear the air, as soon as the situation allowed. If *he* allowed.

She imagined him bristling at the thought, arguing that her foolish social concerns would rob precious minutes from saving the world.

And...he was probably right.

History is also written by the winner.

BY THE time the Helicarrier arrived in Paris airspace, the conference table crowding the lab had been replaced with an equally large monitor array, mounted in front of the quarantine chamber. There was one screen for each of the twelve field agents, three for onsite security-camera feeds, and a sixteenth for a free-flying drone.

Rogers stood pressed against the glass, watching with mixed feelings. Good as it was to be able to do something, studying the drone's distant overhead image made him wish he was on the ground.

Nia and Kade kept their distance, both from the operation and each other. Cap and Fury were essentially free to talk.

"It started as a single triangle that just came out of some stone?"

Fury, leaning heavily against a nearby wall, nodded. "Not just any stone. The Nazis used the Louvre as a clearinghouse for their stolen artwork. After the liberation, that museum came under a lot of scrutiny, so we've got the records. Turns out they were planning to erect a new vault with stones shipped direct from Berlin. It never got built, but one of the blocks wound up being used to carve that little pyramid. Apparently, it already had one side cut at the appropriate angle."

So far, any destruction was an incidental result of the robot's shifting shape. Whenever it changed, the triangles shredded anything in their path, rendering the pavilion too dangerous for local enforcement to do more than evacuate civilians and establish a perimeter.

After configuring itself a dozen ways, the triangles had settled into a headless double-diamond with rising peaks on either side. It spread out so widely, so quickly, that at times it looked as if the Nazis, having once failed to hold Paris, were determined to cover it completely.

Rogers concentrated on the overhead view. "It's been testing itself, trying out its full capacities."

"On the lighter side, unless someone's controlling it remotely, that may be all it ever does," Fury said.

Cap shook his head grimly. "I've fought Nazi robots before. Remember the Sleepers? They didn't need a remote control. They were entombed in a crypt at the bottom of the ocean until the Skull woke them. After that, they acted on their own."

"Sue me for being an optimist, but yeah, you got me there."

"The Nazis made some incredible breakthroughs. The Sleepers may not have had true A.I., but their programming routines were highly sophisticated. Even with an Army unit helping, I couldn't keep the first three from combining. If I hadn't managed to detonate the bomb it carried before it could dig into the earth, it actually might have destroyed the planet." He tapped the glass. "Not that this thing isn't impressive in its own right. How did all that *fit* into one three-foot pyramid?"

"Some kind of compression. Each piece is thousands of times thinner than the original, making them all razor-sharp and a lot less dense. Even so, that little pyramid should've weighed 100 tons. Not only that, resonance imagery is telling us about 10 percent of them are hollow. They're puffed up with some kind of gas, probably created by a chemical reaction when it was activated."

"Gas?"

Before Fury responded, two large shadows appeared on the pavilion. "There are the hover-fliers. Any luck, and a few blasts of good ol' fashioned, unintelligent flying lead will shred the thing."

The familiar voice of the team leader, Agent Jacobs, came over the comm. "Thirty seconds to landing. Good to work with you again, Captain. Kinda the opposite of last time, huh? Can we get a zoom on that overhead?"

Rogers agreed. "Good idea. Move the drone in."

As the drone descended toward the gray metal sea, its high-res image confirmed what the inferior security cameras saw: Each triangle was featureless, perfectly flat. There were no markings, no patterns, no visible variations at all.

As the craft steadied some 10 yards up, the voice boomed out again.

"Wo ist Kapitän Amerika?"

A tendril composed of triangles snapped up toward the drone.

"Evasive action," Rogers said. His order was redundant. The pilot, sitting safely at the controls somewhere on the Helicarrier, was way ahead of him. Its small vertical turbines whining, the drone rose up and away. In comparison, the metallic limb was awkward, clunky in its movements. It looked like an easy escape for the drone—until, as if suddenly realizing its true abilities, the ad-hoc limb shot up.

The screen was briefly covered in dull gray, then went dead.

Dawson *tsked*. "Not the view I was hoping for, but now we know it's responsive to its environment."

Rogers frowned. He didn't like this. The fact that it reacted to the drone and not the civilians meant it was making targeting distinctions. Things could escalate. If he couldn't be there himself, someone like him needed to be.

"Nick, have you contacted any big guns yet?"

"Yeah. Part of protocol. Most of the Avengers are engaged elsewhere, to put it mildly, but someone's on the way. We were just close enough to arrive on scene first."

"Ready to disembark," Jacobs reported.

"Take up positions, but do not engage." That felt as useless as his last command to the drone. He was a relative newcomer to watching a set of screens with his hands tied. Fury, his gaze dancing from monitor to monitor, was the professional.

Rogers decided to focus on Jacobs' feed. Keeping the team leader in mind might make him feel more like he was there.

It did, but as the twelve agents in body armor exited the hoverfliers, he didn't like what he was feeling at all. Having fought dozens of impossible foes, Rogers wanted to treat this like any other unknown. You don't charge in—you probe for reactions, for strengths, for weaknesses, trying to get as much information as possible in exchange for the least risk.

But his gut was telling him different. It was telling him the risk was already too high.

"Let's try the nets."

"All of them?" Jacobs asked.

It was a reasonable question. The S.H.I.E.L.D. electronets delivered

10 times the charge required to knock out a bull elephant. Six could put down the Hulk for a good five minutes; among them, the field agents had twice that number. Unless the construct was purely mechanical, like some kind of giant wind-up toy, the nets wouldn't just fry its wiring—they would melt it.

That would make it harder to study what was left and source its construction, but it would be safer.

"Yes, all of them."

Fury gave him a look, but said nothing.

Swapping sidearms for launchers, the agents took aim. With any luck, the thing would crumple and collapse.

"On my mark. Three…two…one."

Twelve nets soared over the gray field, reaching their apex at nearly the same time. Each fanned into a 10-foot web, pulled down by weights at each corner, as visible energy arced along the strands. The execution was textbook-perfect.

But 12 tendrils rose in response, one beneath each net. Rather than knock them out of the sky as it had the drone, the thing sent more triangles sliding up the tendrils, encasing each net in a crude geodesic dome.

The flash as the nets made contact briefly turned the domes a lighter gray. The powerful charge had some effect: The domes collapsed, and the triangles fluttered downward—but then they were absorbed into the wide surface, seemingly none the worse for wear.

What was left of the nets, charred black, hit the ground soon after.

But the giant killer robot wasn't done. Like a lake responding to a boulder dropped in its center, a large wave headed toward the twelve agents, rending the pavilion as it moved.

"Wo ist Kapitän Amerika?"

It was a recording, yes—but for the first time, Rogers wondered whether the words had any *meaning* for the machine. If it could respond so quickly to their attacks, how much else did it understand about its environment, and its mission?

Fury grunted. "Last I checked, we wo*n* that war, didn't we?"

"Break formation!" Rogers barked. "Give it as many targets as you can! Get to cover, but don't fire! It may not react if it doesn't sense a threat!"

Obeying, the agents scattered, moving away from each other and the quickening metal wave. At first it continued dead ahead. But then it split in pieces, twelve in all, each gaining in speed what had been lost in mass. It was still hard to tell whether they moved by momentum or were being directed—until each curved toward one of the fleeing figures.

Fury tensed and leaned forward. "Damn."

The triangles would reach the slower agents in seconds. A second later, all of them.

Rogers ached to be there, where his enhanced body would make the lag between thought and deed irrelevant. From here, by the time he issued an order, it might be too late.

"We have to distract it with a larger threat. Hover-Flier 1, prepare to fire—"

Before he could finish, the image from Jacobs' feed turned to face the oncoming wall. Close up, the sharp, slashing edges looked like anything but a wave.

"Jacobs, what are you doing?"

"Creating a larger threat."

The barrel of Jacobs' sidearm came into view.

Rogers screamed. "Get out of there!"

There were flashes as the bullets fired, pings and sparks as they bounced off the metal. As if learning, the thing reacted faster this time. The remaining eleven waves turned toward the twelfth, giving the other agents a breather.

Not so Jacobs.

He kept firing. The bullets had no effect. Rogers watched the wall of flashing edges draw closer and closer to Jacobs' open position. The hover-flier was just beginning to rise when Jacobs' screen went black.

Jacobs was down, his condition unknown. The threat gone, the robot was already turning back toward the others. Rogers kept barking orders. "Don't waste this! Evac Plan 2B."

Seeing his pained expression, Fury covered his comm and said, "You'd have done the same."

Rogers covered his. "I might have survived."

Eyes back on the monitors, he watched as the remaining agents began to reach the hover-fliers. "Do *not* lift off! You saw what happened to the drone. Get the pilots out and head for the perimeter."

The teams all but tore the pilots from their seats. The robot reassembled, its pieces quivering, ready for another attack. But, as if it had proven its point, it didn't move.

Rogers switched off his mic again. "If I was there, I could—"

"Infect the world? Imagine how you'd feel then."

"Right. Of course. But this, Fury—watching it all through screens instead of being there—how do you do this every day?"

"Because I have to. Gives you an idea why I don't much care for breaches in the command structure." A loud beeping turned them back to the screens. "Speaking of which, things just might be looking up. Old friend of yours just arrived. I bet you he's not going to listen to orders, either."

A familiar voice came through the comm. "Hey, old man. Heard you got some kind of flu or something, so I figured I'd pitch in."

Rogers' relief was palpable. "Tony?"

If they're gone, no one will fret their questions or ponder their existence. No one except me.

TWO NEW feeds appeared on the monitor array. One showed a line of explosions forming a hot wall between the robot and the fleeing agents. The second showed the face of Tony Stark, the no-longer-a-boy genius who'd inherited his father's looks, brains, company, and wealth. Eyes dancing from point to point to point at his armor's readouts, he occasionally paused to look at the camera.

"Gotta hand it to those Nazi scientists. They really—" he cut himself off. "Nah, on second thought, I don't have to hand them anything. Well, maybe their posthumous ass. Asses? What's the proper grammatical construct here?"

The helter-skelter way he spoke made him seem self-involved and unfocused. Stark was certainly self-involved, but Rogers had figured out long ago that his fellow Avenger was far from unfocused. He was focused on *everything*.

It was just that his mouth had trouble keeping up.

Even his armor's red-and-yellow color scheme had been a careful choice: Iron Man looked like a hurtling flame. The security cameras showed that flame streaking low across the pavilion, firing scores of miniature missiles at the undulating bed of triangles.

Rogers was about to tell him to check on the fallen agent, but Stark beat him to the punch: "Don't contact Mrs. Jacobs just yet. That body armor is better than we thought. He still has a pulse. On it. Hey, Fury, if he pulls through, are you going to reprimand him for disobeying orders or give him a bonus for saving lives?"

"Both," Fury answered, unable to suppress a grin at the news. "Stark, remind me again why you're the only guy who always has a second camera pointed at his kisser?"

As Iron Man snagged Jacobs' still form, his response came quick and easy. "Because I'm *that* handsome? Nah, plenty of posed photos for that."

Rogers voiced the answer they all knew. "Visual intelligence for life support. The suit can practically move on its own, so it's a way to tell if you're still alive in there if the other data feeds fail."

Stark beamed. "See? Ol' Cap gets me."

He hovered to better scan the metal field. The thing still didn't attack, but its pieces gnashed like a thousand metal teeth. When Iron Man drifted lower, Rogers got that feeling in his gut again.

"Careful. It can be pretty quick."

A tendril shot out, still awkward, but faster. Not nearly fast enough, though. Stark slipped to the side so suddenly he seemed to vanish from one spot and reappear in another.

"Like that? Hakuna matata. I was hoping to get that reaction. I couldn't snag the whole thing at once, but now, I can do this."

A stream of energy shot from his palm. Caught in a stasis beam, the triangles creaked and strained against the resistance.

"Not going to hold hands for long, but maybe long enough for my scanners to get a better idea of what makes it tick." After a beat, he spoke again. "Huh. Answer unclear, ask again later. Maybe a Stone Age version of swarm robotics? Here in 2005, we use algorithms to synchronize a swarm, but these puppies seem to operate organically, like the way all those molecules in your eye somehow know they're supposed to be shaped like an eye."

The tendril suddenly lost its form, the pieces tumbling back into the body.

"Oh. Okay. I meant for that to happen. While we're waiting like two seconds for my onboard system to fully process the scans, do we have a name yet for our big isosceles buddy?"

Fury shrugged. "I'm good with 'giant killer robot.'"

"I'll stick with 'the thing,' then. Can't get a handle on the power source, but it's definitely a lot more pianola than microprocessor. All its actions and reactions are a set of predetermined routines."

Tony was the A.I. expert, but Rogers still felt an intelligence present. Maybe it was the designer's intelligence, reflected in crude programming, but it was still an intelligence.

"Just…don't underestimate it. We have to be careful. We need a plan."

Stark rolled his eyes. "Fine. Here's a plan: Blast it to smithereens. I can do a lot better than those nets. They're so last year—I know because I designed them."

Sensing Rogers' frustration, Fury said, "Now you know how I feel when I have to deal with you high-powered types."

Hands out, palms facing down, Stark swooped along the robot's surface. "Fine, fine. Cap's right. Like Dad always said: 'Measure twice, cut once.' Or was it 'Cut first and ask questions later'? Anyway, before I let it rip, I'll do a second scan to make sure there are no surprises—you know, the kind that might explode and harm innocents. Nothing so far, nothing... Whoa."

"Tony? What have you got?"

"Booby trap. Crap. This is so *Testament of Dr. Mabuse*. You know, Fritz Lang? I figured an old guy like you would appreciate the—"

More tendrils burst upwards.

"Oh, I got the reference," Cap said. "Doesn't Mabuse keep coming back?"

"There is that."

Rogers counted six, seven, eight tendrils lurching skyward. He struggled with his desire to help, but there was no need for immediate concern. Like an expert skier slaloming between flags on a slope, Stark twirled among the rising spikes. Failing to reach their target, the tendrils fell back.

"More to the point, the gas those hollow cells are packing? It's Zyklon B, a cyanide compound. It diffuses quickly in the open air, but given the population density and current wind direction, we're talking about five thousand dead before it does."

Once more, the voice boomed out: "*Wo ist Kapitän Amerika?*"

"I'm starting to think it doesn't like me."

This was followed by a roar like a plague of giant insects.

"And now it's engaging another routine, maybe in response to its failure. Or it could have some sort of timer."

The triangles rearranged into shapes like arms, torso, and legs. At the top, it formed a squat structure like the turret on a panzer tank, sans barrel. Rather than follow Iron Man, the spinning turret settled on the centuries-old building across the pavilion. The razor edges of the triangles making up its feet sent chunks of stone flying as it stepped toward the Louvre.

"Guys," Stark said, "tell me the museum's been evacuated."

Fury checked the readout. "Only 75 percent. It's heading away from you. Is it trying to retreat?"

Rogers mind raced. "If it was, why go through the big change? Tony, routine or not, any chance it could be *detecting* the civilians inside?"

The playboy made a face. "Could have a heat sensor. People are hot. I'm hot. The armor, I mean. Well, mostly the armor. But to answer your question, yes."

Turning on his side, Stark sailed between the robot and the building. When he started firing short repulsor blasts, Rogers nearly pounded on the glass. "Tony, the gas!"

"At ease. Not gonna fry it—just giving it a little tickle. Remember what it did when Jacobs shot at it? I just want some of that sweet, sweet attention."

The thing halted. Its turret pivoted, moving just shy of Iron Man's path through the air. Testing its speed, Stark moved up and down, left and right. It imitated the motion for a bit, but then spun back toward the museum.

Another blast from Stark returned its attention.

As he pelted different spots along its form, the head kept spinning, unable to focus.

"My, my! I repeat the attack, it repeats the response. Good. I think I've got it stuck in a loop. Maybe I'll eventually wear down its batteries." Stark grimaced. "Assuming it has batteries."

If it was a loop, there might be something in the pattern they could use. As Iron Man kept up the assault, Rogers studied its reactions. "Whenever you hit a leg, it takes the same step back, then makes the same quarter turn—clockwise on the left, counter-clockwise on the right."

Stark was pleasantly surprised. "Good eyes! So I can steer it. The Seine's right beyond the Louvre. I can get it into the water and blow it up there."

"What about the drinking water?" Rogers asked.

"We're a mile downriver from any pumps, and standard filters can handle it anyway. If you're worried about the fish, we might lose a few in the immediate vicinity, but the river currents will dissipate the cyanide even before it hits the big blue sea."

Soon enough, he had it moving awkwardly backwards. As the blasts came faster, so did the giant's steps. "A little time, a little effort, I could teach it to waltz."

Rogers eyed the maps. "Those three arches at nine o'clock are the *Porte des Lions* entrance. Get it through and you'll be on the *Pont du Carrousel*, which crosses right over the Seine."

"Got it. And may I say, I like your outrageous French accent."

"I spent some time in Paris during the war."

"Which one? Oh yeah, right…"

Fury leaned closer to the screens. "That wing's been cleared, but all the same, try not to hurt the museum full of priceless art, okay?"

Rogers shook his head. "Don't give it any more time than you have to. For all we know it's got a pre-programmed routine to get out of this—it's just accessing it slowly."

Stark *harrumphed.* "Go slow, go fast. Geez. Backseat drivers."

As Iron Man aimed the plodding giant toward the arches, Fury addressed his teams. "Okay everybody, our job is to make sure Shell-Head and his dance partner get an unobstructed path. Alpha-one, clear local enforcement from those arches. Alpha-two, make sure there isn't any traffic on that bridge."

After that, save for the sounds of the blasts, the rush of Iron Man's thrusters, and the heavy tread of the triangles, the lab fell silent. The turret continued to dog its attacker. Unable to lock on, the thing kept lumbering toward the arches. Slavishly, its pseudo-legs continued responding to the precisely aimed blasts until it neared a final, tight turn. As it backed beneath the central arch, the turret hit the stone.

A rain of fist-sized rocks clattered along its surface.

"Stark!"

"Save the guff for the grunts, Colonel. I bet Cap thinks I'm doing a great job, right, Cap?"

Rogers noticed a bit of sweat on Stark's temple. "You're doing fine, Tony."

With every additional step, it became less likely the thing would change routines. Even so, all three men held their breath, relaxing only slightly when it emerged from the shadow of the arch onto a wide, empty avenue.

"That was tougher than I thought. Kind of like parallel parking in the city during rush hour—with your eyes closed."

On the far bank, the Parisian police were doing their best to keep a growing crowd behind the hastily arranged roadblocks. As the strange colossus stomped onto the bridge, even the officers took a moment to stare at it and the fiery gnat showering it with bursts of blue light.

When at last it reached the edge of the bridge, Stark fired a final time. "Nowhere to go but down."

It stepped back, as it had dozens of times before, but now the foot landed on air. As it teetered, the torso twisted, attempting to recapture its lost balance—but it wasn't quite fast enough. The robot tumbled toward the river.

Stark's loud exhale was picked up by the speakers. "Whew! Now we just have to hope it doesn't—"

A din of clicking interrupted him. Its body flattened as it fell. It dipped below the water only to bob back to the surface, its turret intact and turning.

"Damn. The fall itself must have engaged a different routine. Probably has some sort of a gyroscope to help it keep its balance."

The colossus spoke again:

"Wenn Kapitän Amerika ist nicht hier innerhalb einer stunde, werden viele zivilisten sterben."

"Whoa. A *really* different routine."

The translation appeared on their screens: "If Captain America is not here within an hour, many civilians will die."

Undulating on the river's surface, it moved toward the crowded far bank. Hoping to change its direction, Iron Man blasted it, but it now ignored him. He dove beneath the river's surface, firing at it along the way in the hopes that it might follow him into the Seine. No luck: It continued toward the bank.

"Why didn't it follow you?" Fury asked.

"The new routine is overriding the old one. So to recap, if I try to fry it, people die. If I do nothing, people die. Unless Steve shows up, that's it for multiple choice, and there's no 'None of the Above.' So exactly how bad *is* this bug you've got, Cap?"

I'll be the only one deciding what they are worth.
So why shouldn't I decide if they live?

FURY scowled. "A virus inactive for years versus an imminent gas attack? There aren't any good choices, but maybe we could wrap you in one of our fancy hazmat suits long enough for you to introduce yourself."

Try as Nia might to focus on her work, her ears perked. She watched the conflicting emotions on the First Avenger's face. Clearly, he wanted to jump on the chance, but the decision wasn't his. As if sensing her attention, he called out, "Doctors? You want to weigh in?"

She hesitated, waiting for Kade to speak first, but he didn't. Despite the drama playing out on the multiple flatscreen monitors, he remained absorbed by the molecular holograms floating before him.

She cleared her throat. "Dr. Kade? Under the circumstances, how would you feel about Captain Rogers wearing a combat hazmat suit?"

He looked up absently. "That's not necessary. As long as he stays in the containment chamber..."

Nudging him sharply, she nodded toward the monitors. The cold voice again came through the speakers:

"*Wo ist Kapitän Amerika?*"

His face dropped. "Absolutely not. NO! You can't send him into a fight!"

Fury fought to keep his voice even. "Doc, I'm sure you know that ever since Iraq, the DOD's been ramping up the effectiveness of their hazmat suits. What I hope you don't know, since it's supposed to be secret, is that we have something even more advanced." He pressed a few buttons on his PDA. "I'm sending you and Dr. N'Tomo the specs now, but I'm gonna need an answer fast if we're going to get Cap there by the deadline."

Kade was apoplectic. "Are you all *insane?*"

Nia's hand on his shoulder only made things worse. "Can we have a minute?"

Fury held up a finger. "One minute. One."

Kade let her lead him into the corridor, but pulled away the moment the door hissed shut. "Why bother with this charade when it's clear you'll just override me again?"

She responded with the practiced calm she used on panicking patients. "When circumstances change, the arguments have to change along with them. The virus has been present for years, but this...giant killer robot...will make good on its threat in an hour. That's thousands of real deaths versus a theory."

Kade tried to control himself. "Those deaths are just as theoretical. What's not theoretical is the fact that thirty-six *thousand* people die yearly from the *flu*. That's infinitesimal compared to what this virus might do to our species."

Feeling lectured, she crossed her arms over her chest. "*Might*, but we have absolutely no way to know the odds of it suddenly activating."

Kade hissed. "Absent an understanding of what keeps it in check, of course not. We only know what will happen if it does!"

She lowered her voice, a simple trick she usually used on children. "But we *do* understand exactly what's keeping the gas in check, what it's asking for, and what it's threatening to do if it doesn't get that.."

Kade stiffened. "That's exactly what these cowboys with their adolescent sense of heroics are saying. As I suspected, you've already made your decision. I won't waste time on what I can't control. But if Rogers' blood is scattered on the Paris streets and humanity dies as a result, the fault will be yours, Dr. N'Tomo, not mine!"

TWENTY minutes later, Steve Rogers was in the drone hover-flier, Nia checking his hazmat suit over and over again. Catching his reflection in a silver strut, he was reminded of a toddler immobilized by his first snow-jumper. The full-head helmet and thick goggles were awkward, but his strength and speed should more than compensate for the bulkiness.

"This won't tear if I move too quickly, will it?"

Nia, in her own suit, tightened a shoulder strap, then loosened it again. "The composite fabric has a tensile strength similar to Kevlar. It won't stop a bullet, but it should stand up to your combat acrobatics."

"I appreciate your coming along for this."

She kept working. "Just so you know, the suit won't help much if the gas is released. I reversed the filters to purify the air when you exhale, to protect the populace from…"

Her voice trailed off—whether from emotion, or a tricky buckle, he wasn't sure.

"The virus. I know."

Her hand moved from the shoulder strap to the star on his chest. The hazmat suit had been hastily painted to resemble the uniform he wore beneath. "Funny how they worried you *would* be recognized in Somalia. Now they're worried you won't be."

"Price of fame?"

She didn't smile. "Paris isn't the desert, but it will feel like over 100 degrees in there. Your metabolism is four times normal, so you'll need four times the water to stay hydrated. There's a retractable straw near mouth level. Make sure you use it." She looked up at him with her sharp, intelligent eyes. "You do sweat, don't you?"

He nodded.

Fury's voice came over the comm. "Drop off in 60 seconds. Time for the doctor to strap in."

Positioning herself in the safety harness, she said, "I wish there was more I could do. If I weren't an atheist, I'd pray."

The rear hatch opened. Beneath a light cover of clouds, the streets of Paris were visible.

"There are no atheists in foxholes," Cap said.

The engine roared louder, but he heard her response through his comm. "Just so you know, Steve, that's not an argument against atheism. It's an argument against foxholes."

He turned to make the jump. "Didn't James Morrow say that?"

Ears filling with a rush of air, Rogers barely heard her answer yes as he threw himself into the sky. Back arched, limbs together for the long descent, he watched the scene on the ground grow larger. S.H.I.E.L.D. and local enforcement had pushed the crowd back, but he could see hundreds of cars locked in traffic just a few blocks away.

As gravity drew him nearer, he made out the glint of the robot's metal and the streak of hot air that followed Iron Man's movements. Stark was trying to keep the thing in the water by blasting away the stone support wall along the bank. He was only partly successful. Its tendrils reached over the bank and wrapped around several tree trunks to pull itself up.

The sound of the blasts became audible, then the clicking of the triangles, and finally Stark on the comm: "My, my. Cap's got himself a lady friend."

"Shut up, Tony." He pulled the ripcord, releasing the chute.

"Cap and Nia sitting in a tree…"

"Tony…"

"Hey, I think it's a good thing. Anything that loosens you up. So what's the play?"

Cap's descent slowed. He used the parachute cords to steer toward the bridge. "Making it up as I go along. It wants to meet me, so I guess the first step is to announce myself."

With no one certain *how* the robot would be able to recognize him, his comm was linked to a speaker system in the suit. When he activated it, his voice boomed louder than the dead *Führer's* recording.

"You wanted me, here I am!"

Yanking his shield from his back, he tossed it at the largest tendril. It hit with a loud thunk. The shock waves briefly disturbed the pattern of the triangles as the shield returned to his hand.

The moment his feet touched down on the bridge, Cap released the chute and pivoted to the water to see whether the strike, or his presence, had any additional effect.

Not quite sure how to address the giant killer robot, he called out, "I don't know who sent you, but if you don't stand down immediately, you will be destroyed!"

He felt a little silly threatening something that likely didn't understand him. But according to Stark, the more he spoke, the better the chance its voice-recognition functions, if it had any, would kick in.

So far, other than reassembling its tendril, the thing hadn't moved. He stepped to the edge of the bridge. "Can you hear me? This is—"

"Kapitän Amerika, machen sie sich bereit zu sterben!"

He'd heard that in German often enough. *Captain America, prepare to die!*

The chittering of its pieces melted into a single metallic moan. Now flat, it veered toward him, sliding across the water.

Stark hovered behind it. "Standing by, Steve. You're the one it wants, you call the shots."

"Don't do anything yet. As long as it's moving away from the bank, I want its attention on me."

"Roger that, Rogers."

"This sound system's pretty good, Tony. Did you hear me rolling my eyes at that?"

"Indeed I did."

One foot on the bridge's stone wall, shield in hand, Rogers watched the robot coalesce into something akin to a ship with a tall angular prow. Three tower-like structures rose clumsily from its center. The change in its weight distribution made it tilt one way, then another, but it did not slow down.

Near the bridge supports, the trio of towers bent forward. Given what it had tried to do with the trees along the bank, Cap expected it to use the towers to pull itself onto the bridge.

But it didn't. It froze, bobbing in the water.

He called to it again. "I'm right here. What are you waiting for?"

He heard more clicking and clacking, but it had stopped bobbing. The angled towers should have tipped it over, but it was steady. It had to be bracing itself from beneath.

By the time he realized why, it was almost too late. It was readying for an attack. Scores of spinning triangles erupted from the towers. Some drove through the stone at his feet. Others rained around him, shredding asphalt and concrete.

Weaving between the deadly missiles, Rogers leapt back and hit the ground, rolling out of the way. By the time he got to his feet, there wasn't much room left to stand.

The entire bridge was collapsing.

As Steve jumped along the tumbling concrete and exposed rebar, Stark spoke through the comm. "Okay, so in this case, past performance is not the best indicator of future behavior. You're gonna want to head to the Louvre side. More of that area's been evacuated. There is all that precious art, though."

"Still don't think it's an A.I.?"

"No. Don't *want* to think so, anyway. My guess is the programmer had something special planned for you. Want help?"

"Not yet."

"Your funeral...uh, party. Your party. Let's go with that."

A second barrage, thicker than the first, forced Cap to twist midair. As he made for the remaining section of bridge, a triangle caught him near the thigh, slicing through several layers of the hazmat suit.

He had to end this fight quickly. But how?

He leapt toward the triangles that remained anchored in the water. The missile attacks had diminished the height of the three towers, but even now the fired pieces returned, clicking back into place.

Below him, what seemed a flat surface revealed itself to be a series of tightly packed edges. If he hit it at his current speed, the suit wouldn't be the only thing shredded. Pressing the curve of his shield toward the robot, Cap curled his body against it for protection. Wild sparks flew as he skimmed along the sharp surface.

He'd survived another few seconds. Now what?

Whether or not it could think, its designer had gone through a lot of trouble planning to destroy not just anyone, but *him*, Captain America.

"Tony, I'm going for a swim. If it follows, you know what to do. Don't wait for me to surface."

"Wait! Aside from not wanting you to die, I've got another problem with that. I already tried it, and it didn't work, remember?"

He jumped. "That's because you're not me."

"No need to get all superior. Oh, I get it. *I'm* not its target."

The hazmat suit not only made for an awkward dive, but when he went under, the murky water started seeping through the reversed gas-mask filters, obscuring his goggles and forcing him to hold his breath. Nonetheless, he kicked and stroked, driving his heavy body deeper, until he felt the current tug him beneath the bridge.

He turned onto his back, hoping to see the robot before the mask filled up completely. "Follow me, damn it! Follow me!"

"You kiss that nice doctor with that mouth?" came Tony's voice. "Looks like you were right. It's reverting to a denser version of that turret configuration and letting itself sink."

A low, muffled roar rumbled from above. The sunlight, already dim below the river's surface, darkened further. Cap saw it coming now, its shape still changing, its gray rendered black. A few triangles shot past him, torpedo-like, leaving trails of bubbles in their wake. The fact that they missed made him feel more lucky than safe. He turned over and swam, forcing himself deeper.

"Once it's completely under, Tony, give it all you've got."

"Uh, Cap, remember my first objection? The suit protects me from energy discharges, but not you. If I let loose with major voltage, and you're anywhere near, you're gonna—"

"Just do it!" As he spoke, the gritty water filled his mouth.

"Okay, but do me a favor and try to put some distance between you and the 'bot. Swim with the current, not against it—that sort of thing."

Already swimming as fast as he could, he spit out the grit and kept working his arms and legs. Remembering Nia's advice, he sucked some fresh water into his mouth through the straw. It was warm, but clean.

When he paused to look back, he saw more spinning triangles headed his way. Before he could try to avoid them, a wide crackle of bluish light blinded him. The loud rumble that followed so rattled and filled him, he wasn't sure where it began and he ended. After that, he wasn't sure of anything at all.

The next thing he sensed were Stark's armored hands lifting him, pulling him through the water and out into the air. He wanted to see what had happened, but the hazmat goggles were hopelessly clouded. He reached for the helmet to remove it, but heard Tony's warning through the comm.

"Orders are to leave the helmet on until you're sealed in the hover-flier."

Exhausted, he nodded. The hands let go. With a clunk, he landed on hard metal and heard the hatch seal shut.

Nia, still in her own suit, helped him remove the helmet. "This is against protocol, but that glass is pretty cracked anyway, and the hover-flier environment is sealed. Dr. Kade would doubtless disagree, but I don't see any harm in letting you have a quick look."

He stared out the rear window. Below, pieces of the robot floated in clumps on the surface of the Seine. They still clicked against one another, but only when the currents happened to push them together.

"You did it," Nia said softly. Then she covered his head with a spare helmet.

10

If something's about to destroy you, the obvious choice is to destroy it first.

JOHANN Schmidt was increasingly upset—not at the result of the battle, but by the fact he had to watch it the same way as the rest of the masses: on the news. He'd hoped the Sonikey might link him to a camera placed within the Sleeper, but apparently that technology wasn't available for *Der Führer*'s little hidden project.

It might've been, had Hitler thought to consult him. Their advances in mechanical television had been considerable.

All the same, the Skull wondered, why was he feeling so strangely petty when he should be pleased and impressed? The mysterious manner in which the hard, lightweight pieces interconnected left even Zola looking like a child watching his first magic trick. It had been a long time since Schmidt had reason to admire Hitler or his Reich.

Instead, he couldn't help but wonder what other secrets had been kept from him.

The press had been allowed beyond the cordon. The reports from the scene sounded more prerecorded than Hitler's voice:

"We're live from the Seine, where, moments ago, a stunning battle took place in the heart of Paris. We're just hearing now that the hazmat suit Captain America wore may have been a precaution against a potential gas attack from the…"

Hairless brow furrowing, he muted the report. "Arnim, do you recall any other situations where Rogers made such a garish effort to protect himself?"

Zola's synthetic voice issued from the speakers on his shoulders. "I do not."

Schmidt's eyes widened. "Then…?"

"Yes. The logical conclusion is that Rogers has the virus, too. It's possible it was inadvertently replicated when I created the clone."

The revelation thrilled Schmidt. "And it is killing him, too?"

"Not currently. As you saw, he fought as well as ever. His capacities were not diminished in any way; therefore he is not symptomatic."

Disappointment made him spit as he asked, "How, if our bodies are identical?"

"Perhaps because they are not identical any longer. The clone *was* identical to Steve Rogers, but only in the moment the sample was procured. Ever since, you've lived separate lives, earned different scars. The Dust of Death that disfigured you, for instance, may have compromised your immune system. Or perhaps the virus mutated into a more active strain inside you—mutating is what viruses do, after all. Another possibility is that he has the same virus, but S.H.I.E.L.D. has found a way to keep his symptoms in check. If so, *Herr* Skull, it's in the interest of all humans to keep the virus from spreading. You might want to consider contacting them."

The Skull's already plank-stiff figure tightened. "So they can keep me imprisoned in quarantine until I die? So I can become the guinea pig who enables them to save their great hero? I don't think so."

For a while, the Skull had been working to suppress a cough. Each time he succeeded, it felt like a small triumph, but now a powerful spasm caught him off-guard. Shoulders heaving, he hacked until every last ounce of air was expelled from his wheezing lungs.

When it was over, he straightened again. The spattered flecks of blood were barely noticeable against the red of his cheeks and chin, but when he wiped his lips with his black-gloved hands, the droplets glowed like tiny rubies. Tremors ran along his fingers. Schmidt wiped his glove, then wrapped the handkerchief around his hand to stop its shaking.

"In the orphanage where I was raised, several of the children had consumption. I'd spend my idle hours watching them suffer. Some fought, battling to suck in air. Others meekly surrendered. Their attitude made little difference in how long they lived. Still, I considered those who chose to give in to be weaker."

"Any comparison to the virus is not apt. Pulmonary tuberculosis is caused by a bacteria that focuses on the lungs."

The genetic engineer had always possessed an irritating form of objectivity, but this response was so mechanical, Schmidt wondered how much of himself Zola had given up when he occupied that machine. But then the avatar in the android's chest tilted. Lines formed little furrows along the forehead and brow as the lips pursed and crinkled. It looked almost sad.

"I am sorry the Sleeper was destroyed, that your plan has failed."

The Skull's response was a rasping hiss. "It did not fail!"

The android gestured at the screens. "But Rogers was not only victorious—the wreckage is being recovered by S.H.I.E.L.D."

A high-pitched tone filled the room. It had no effect on the android, but it burrowed into Schmidt's head, making his teeth ache. At least it wasn't some new symptom. At least he knew what it was.

The Sonikey was humming.

"There, you see? They weren't codenamed *Sleeper* solely because of the time that might pass before their use. Once acquiring the necessary data, each is programmed to play dead, to go dormant until its siblings complete their tasks. And now, the second awakens."

Despite what it meant, the harsh sound jangled his nerves. He struggled to focus, squeezing the balled handkerchief in his fist tighter and tighter until the sensation conjured another feeling: not silk, but flesh, soft and yielding.

He saw the startled face of Esther, the Jewish shopkeeper's daughter, the girl who'd evoked his passions and then rejected him. Strangling her was the first time he'd fully released his rage. She, like those sheep at the orphanage who gave themselves up to their disease, had simply surrendered. Ever since, the ecstasy of that sensation had informed his being. Before he'd ever met Hitler, that moment told him who he was.

"Arnim, I find myself...oddly sentimental."

"I am beginning to think the virus is affecting your limbic system. It is the seat of emotion and memory."

"Ach. That would explain it."

The memory of her bulging eyes held him until the vibrations of the Sonikey ceased. As the Skull tossed the handkerchief into a wastebasket, her dying face vanished.

Suddenly, he could not recall her at all. She became just a name—a name linked to a dull, distant ache that conjured neither sight nor sound.

But is it so easy to destroy if it's the most astonishing thing you've ever seen?

EVEN the hardiest urban explorer considered Belgium's Clabecq Iron Foundry, closed since 1992, extremely dangerous. But every corner of the world had its bored teens, youths who either didn't care, didn't believe, or willfully ignored their own mortality—and the occasional campfires that licked the rusting structures often went unnoticed.

Quinten was about to toss another wood scrap on the fire when Brent grabbed his hand. "What?"

"Don't make it too big. The guards will see."

"You're boss now?"

Most of the others were busy texting or bobbing their heads to the music playing through their earbuds. Amelie was paying attention, though. Quinten smiled at her, then nodded at the wavering darkness. "Where? What guards?"

Slightly older, Brent took the vague challenge in stride. "They can't afford to hire many, but trust me, they're out there. Why ruin a good thing? Keep the fire low."

Quinten grimaced, but chucked the wood into the shadows.

Amelie, in shorts and midriff, moved closer. She sat cross-legged and rubbed her hands over the fire, pretending to be cold. "Don't pout, Quinten. After all, Brent found the statues, didn't he?"

"But we all worked to get them out of the crates." He put his head in her lap, and looked up at the two bronze forms. Once the statues were unpacked, the little group of outcasts tried to get them to face each another, so the orbs each figure held would touch and form a sort of protective shrine. But they were too heavy.

"The Nazis made them, you know," Brent said. "There were swastikas airbrushed onto those boards."

Quinten was right below one of the spheres, so that whenever the firelight flickered the right way, he could make out the carved fingernails on the cupped hands. "They were too rotted to tell for sure."

Still not happy with the fire's glow, Brent took out another piece of wood. "They were swastikas."

Quinten rolled his eyes. "Fine. Swastikas."

Amelie looked up into the bronze faces. "How could something so beautiful come from something so ugly?"

Quinten smirked. "You came from your parents, didn't you?"

She grabbed him by the cheeks and shook his face, the way his mother used to when he said something out of line. "Don't be terrible."

Worried he might ruin things with her, Quinten tried to enjoy the quiet, but Brent started talking again. "Definitely Nazis. Who do you think they're supposed to be? Why are they holding those globes?"

"Gods, maybe? I don't know." Quinten shifted in Amelie's lap. "If they're Nazi, how did they get all the way here? Belgium was occupied, but…"

Amelie glared. "Stop talking. Stop thinking, both of you. Try to be in the moment. Shh."

Brent eyed her. "Aren't you even curious?"

She stroked Quinten's hair. "No. If you listen quietly, you can hear the wind make the buildings creak."

Quinten looked into her eyes until she closed them, then decided to do the same. All he heard was the crackling firewood. Bored, he was about to say something when he caught a heavier sound. It was close—too close to be the settling of the sheet-metal walls against their rusting steel supports. It didn't sound like metal, anyway—more like stone rubbing stone.

But even that wasn't quite right. It wasn't stone, exactly.

And it was getting louder.

He opened his eyes—and kept opening them until they refused to grow any wider. The statue's arms were lowering. It looked as if it had come to life, until the scar-like rifts forming along its shoulders revealed that it was simply collapsing—right on top of them.

Terrified, he rolled, pulling Amelie along with him. The others popped to their feet, scrambling to get away.

"Run!" Quinten screamed. His cry was nearly drowned out by the thud of the massive sphere and arms hitting the concrete. As it echoed and the dust settled, the panicked teens stopped to stare.

Brent, who'd been the last to run, took a few cautious steps back toward the stone figures.

When the three-meter sphere rolled over him, it made a sound completely unlike metal or stone.

This time it was Amelie who screamed and ran. Quinten kept staring. The sphere was part of a statue, not alive. It shouldn't do that. It wasn't possible. It hadn't even started off slowly, the way a car accelerated. One moment it was still, the next moving.

As it kept rolling, a panting Amelie called from somewhere in the dark. "Quinten! Why aren't you running?"

Her voice, usually so familiar, sounded strange and harsh, as if from a dream. Part of him wasn't sure any of this was real. Maybe he *was* dreaming. It took the dead, hollow tones from the moving sphere to finally snap him into the moment:

"Ich komme um zu töten Kapitän Amerika."

Quinten spun and pressed his feet into the concrete floor. He took off. The sphere kept a straight course: not turning, not speeding, and not slowing down. Even when it hit the wall, its direction didn't change. The sheet metal buckled, fell, and flattened as the orb passed over it.

The sphere wasn't chasing them at all. Poor Brent had simply been standing in the wrong spot.

LESS than an hour later, Quinten sat shivering under a blanket, surrounded by men and women in dark uniforms. They said they were police, but they didn't look like any police he'd ever seen. He overheard one say that "Colonel Fury" had been informed, but the name meant nothing to him. They'd corralled Quinten and his friends and separated them, claiming it was to keep their stories from influencing one another.

All Quinten wanted to do was find out whether Amelie was okay. When they'd been nabbed, she had been so terrified she started hyperventilating. They said she was fine, that she was receiving medical attention, but they wouldn't let him see her.

Instead, they peppered him with questions. They asked why the teens hadn't reported finding the crates in the first place, as if that meant they were somehow in on their secrets.

"Because we're stupid teenagers, why do you think?"

Prodding, they told him about the dead millionaire who'd hid the statues here after the war. They wondered whether the man was a Nazi sympathizer, or, as his public statements said, just a fan of the sculptor—as if Quinten might somehow know.

Of course, he didn't!

He was so exhausted, he couldn't even bring himself to care about the history of the statues, that one represented the Greek titan Atlas supporting the heavens, and the other the Roman goddess Tellus supporting the earth. They were to be part of a *Volkshalle* in the New Berlin the Nazis imagined, some huge domed building intended for the public worship of Hitler.

Brent would have cared about all of that. But Brent was dead.

When Quinten shook and began to sob, they gave him some water and told him he'd be released soon—after a few more questions.

Yes, he'd seen the news story about the battle in Paris. No, he hadn't made any connection between that and the sphere until they made it for him.

"Was that exactly what it said? *Ich komme um zu töten Kapitän Amerika?* I come to kill Captain America?"

"Yes. I think. Yes. Please, I want to—"

"It didn't ask *where* Captain America was? Why not?"

"How should I know? Maybe it already knows where he is!"

How do you decide if it's worth the risk?

ROGERS had been back in quarantine only a few hours when word of the sphere reached the Helicarrier. The fight at the Louvre had satisfied a physical itch, putting his mind more at ease. He leaned on the glass of his chamber almost casually as he and Fury studied the real-time satellite imagery.

"Are we ready to call it a Sleeper, yet?" he asked.

Fury pointed at the red line originating in Belgium. "There sure as hell is some kind of familial thing going on. Same recorded voice, same material, same taste in basic shapes. You piss off some geometry teacher when you were a kid?"

"Sorry. I always handed in my homework on time."

"Figures." The red line grew longer. "But this second Sleeper isn't calling you out—it's headed straight for you. Anything it can't roll over it, it goes through. So far, that includes three farmhouses, a corporate center, and a train station. Civilian authorities are trying to clear a path, but they're under orders not to engage. Somehow or other, it knows where you are."

Stark strolled in, his rumpled civvies doing nothing to dampen his self-assurance. "You sure about that, Fury?"

Cap looked at him. "I'm surprised you're not already out there. I'd be if I could."

Tony tapped his forehead. "Know thy enemy. Rather than set off any defenses, I'm trying to get a better handle on how exactly these things work, which is proving, well...*insane* is a good word. It looks like a smooth, featureless sphere, but it has to have some sort of mechanism inside, right? All I really know is that it's giving off a weak, steady radio-frequency signal. Even if I buy that it's using that for some sort of echolocation, isolating your biometrics at this distance would be like cavemen using wooden cudgels to find the Higgs boson. That's why I can't wrap my head around the idea that it's tracking you."

Fury crossed his arms. "Actually, I wasn't sure either, until I had our heading slightly changed three times, like you asked. Each time, the sphere adjusted course to match."

Tony looked genuinely bewildered. "Damn. Okay, it's following *something*, but what if it's not Cap? Maybe there's a transmitter hidden in all that killer-robot wreckage you've got stowed in the hover-flier."

"Beat you to that one. I sent the hover-flier about 100 miles away. Nothing. And before you ask, we scoured Steve, the uniform, the shield, the hazmat suit, the other two heli-jets, and all the field agents who were on the ground. No signals in or out, no sign of anything resembling a bug. I'll say it again: Somehow, that thing knows where Cap is."

Intellectual puzzles usually tickled the playboy. This one seemed to frighten him. His darting eyes reminded Rogers of Kade, in a way. "Fine. Sleeper Two knows, but Sleeper One had to ask. If it didn't plant something *on* him, it must've gotten something *from* him—a way to ID him—and passed that along before it was destroyed." Stopping short, he looked up at the ceiling. "Wait, wait, wait. Is this really a bad thing?"

"I'm going with…yes?" Rogers said.

"Hear me out. If it *can* track you, that makes the big issue, what? Location, location, location. Take the Helicarrier over the ocean. If it throws itself in, we zap it like the first one—no fuss, no muss."

Steve raised an eyebrow. "I can't help but think the Nazis would have planned for something like water."

Fury shrugged. "It's followed us this far already. At least we can try to lead it away from major population centers. I'll have the helm take us over the Atlantic at full speed. The less time we give this thing to get any new ideas, the better."

Satisfied with himself once more, Stark slapped his hands. "That was easy. Now I'll cure this virus thing, and after lunch, world hunger. Sound like a plan?"

Before the others could crack a smile, Dr. Kade stormed in. The hazmat suit was under his arms.

"*This* was the best you had?"

Stark put out his hand. "Dr. Kade, I assume? I see the stories about your witty repartee were not exaggerated."

Ignoring him, Kade threw the suit across the nearest lab counter, fanning it like a tablecloth so it could be seen in its entirety. Until that moment, Rogers thought the combat had gone reasonably well. The multitude of cuts along the protective fabric, large and small, said otherwise. Each had a numbered tag. The lowest number he could make out was 162.

There were at least 162 rips in the suit.

Fury reached toward it, but hesitated.

Kade hissed at him. "No need to worry *now*, Colonel. I had it sterilized. If the virus can survive 200 degrees Celsius and the chemical bath I used, we're doomed no matter what we do."

The opening door turned them toward Nia N'Tomo, panting. She'd apparently been chasing Kade.

"They seem to prefer you, N'Tomo, so you tell them. A fraction of an inch and we'd be trying to sift his blood from the Seine!"

She paused to catch her breath. "That's accurate, but you're leaving out the fact that the suit actually held."

As she approached, Stark adjusted his wrinkled shirt. "Just so you know, I could do that—sift his blood from the Seine. It wouldn't be easy. Might take…maybe six months, but the unique genetic markers from the Super-Soldier serum would make it a lot easier to pinpoint. Kind of like using gamma radiation to locate…"

Kade interrupted. "And if he'd been cut *above* the water? How long would it take you to filter all the air in Paris?"

Stark frowned. "Longer."

Nia ran her fingertips along the largest tear, inserting her index finger. "The suit has multiple layers. The final layer is the strongest, and as long as it remained intact…" Exerting barely any pressure, her nail pierced what was left of the fabric and came out the other side.

She fell silent.

Satisfied his point had been made, Kade looked at Rogers. "We can't let you out again. You understand that, don't you? If anything, we should be focused on getting you into a cryo-chamber as soon as the situation permits."

Nia rubbed the single thread that had clung to her nail. "I have to agree."

Rogers stared at the suit. Had he been selfish? "Maybe there was another way, but I couldn't see it."

"The end of the world's been a lot closer than a ripped tuxedo," Stark said. "You know that. All you did was save a lot of lives."

Cap sat on the edge of the exam table. "I appreciate what you're trying to say, Tony, but this is different. Being stuck here was driving me crazy. I wanted to be out there doing what I've always done—fighting. Those instincts always served me well, but now they could endanger billions. If that happened, I'd never forgive myself."

Kade lowered his voice. "You needn't concern yourself with guilt. If the virus became active, you'd most likely be dead, too."

Stark bristled. "Whoa, ease up on the war hero, okay?"

Kade looked puzzled. "It was meant as a comfort."

The two stared at each other, brows identically twisted. It was as if both men were unsure whether they were encountering some strange new species, or staring at a funhouse mirror.

Hand cupped to his ear, Fury snapped his fingers and pointed at the largest screen on the array.

Rogers saw why immediately. "The sphere stopped."

Still listening, the colonel kept his head down. "Yeah, right when we hit max speed."

Stark's joking tone gave way to urgency. "Head back over Europe, now. Right now. I know you think it's oh-so-smart, but trust me, these Sleepers have a real limited repertoire. It senses Cap, it heads toward him. If it doesn't, it will hit its next routine…"

The poorly recorded voice that came across the speakers was as familiar as its words: *"Wenn Kapitän Amerika ist nicht hier inner-halb einer stunde, werden viele zivilisten sterben."*

"Right. That routine right there. Many civilians will die. Never mind. Too late. We know what the last one planned to do when it didn't get what it wanted."

Rogers looked to Nia and Kade. "We could use all the help we can get. Any suggestions?"

Still holding the torn suit, Nia said, "Anything can be fooled. Viruses survive by fooling the body. There must be some way to fool this Sleeper."

Kade tilted his head. "If it's identifying you through things like heart rate, metabolism, and body temperature, those would be negligible in stasis. Once we freeze you, it might not be able to detect you anymore."

Stark briskly shook his head. "That might've worked *before* it initiated the new routine, but not now. Now it's all tick-tick-tick, get Cap or kill people. We have to give it Steve Rogers." He scratched at his goatee as if the solution might be found between the hair follicles. *"But...*flip that around. Fool it the other way. Give it something it *thinks* is Steve Rogers. I could use the Iron Man suit to mimic Cap's biometrics. It could even use his voice, his tactics."

Kade prickled. "He can't go out again! He..."

Stark grabbed Kade by the shoulders and gave him a grin. "No, no, no, you beautiful bastard. He stays right here, in quarantine, operating the suit by remote. Hey, Cap, ever play any video games?"

But why would I ever value anything more than myself?

THE RED-AND-YELLOW armor streaked toward the octagon of open sky at the end of the Helicarrier bay.

"Looking good, just hold it steady."

Slightly off-center, the figure tried to correct its path and head for the free air. Instead, it made a sharp turn and slammed the last support beam. Insulted, the girder snapped. One piece dangled precariously. The other tumbled to the bay floor.

Twirling like a child's pinwheel caught in a hurricane, the Iron Man armor careened into the clouds.

"Lower the... Push the... No, not that one... Just..."

Back in Lab 247, it was clear that virus or no, Stark wanted to reach through the glass and grab the controls from Steve Rogers. As his precious armor flipped end over end, his fingers jabbed a few buttons on his own console.

"I've activated the auto-stabilizers. It won't give you the same road-feel, but let go of the thrust lever anytime you get in trouble, and it'll level you out with your head up—whatever your position or velocity. Do that. Do it now, please."

Rogers lifted his index finger. The suit twisted, rose, and slowed. "Are we sure this is a good idea?"

"Nope," Fury answered. "I'm sure it's a terrible idea. But it does have the advantage of being the *only* idea we've got."

Rogers wished he'd taken up one of the many invitations he'd gotten to spend an evening playing one of the latest action video games. Until today, given his lifestyle, the idea had struck him as redundant.

"Tony, you don't use the armor yourself this way much, do you?"

Satisfied that the suit had survived and the Helicarrier wasn't losing altitude, Stark indulged in a final little shiver. "Not if I don't have to. The controls are intuitive, and the armor's onboard systems can second-guess you half the time—or at least second-guess *me*—but it's not the same as being there."

"What if I accidentally fire a missile or a repulsor at the wrong target?"

"You can't. I've adjusted the parameters so you can *only* shoot the Sleeper, and then only if there's nothing organic between you and it. That little trick, I admit, I *do* use when civilians are around. Okay, I'm going to take a deep breath, then I want you to try leveling off and giving us a little, you know, *swoop* back in the Helicarrier's general direction."

Rogers looked at the series of buttons, levers, and dials surrounding the HUD. He moved the correct control slightly. The suit shot past the Helicarrier, narrowly missing one of its four giant propulsion fans.

"No, no! Back off. Fury, are there any civilian aircraft less than a thousand miles away that he could hit?"

"We're clear."

Rogers sighed and released the lever. The suit slowed and hovered. Every time he thought he was getting a feel for it, he nearly destroyed something.

"Even with my reflexes, this will take some training."

"Not a luxury we have," Fury explained. "We're about ten minutes from the Sleeper's location."

Stark eyed the controller hungrily. "Look, the suit's already transmitting a simulation of all your beautiful biometrics, and just in case the Sleeper's got some kind of facial-recognition thing, your face is being projected on top of the helmet. Maybe I should steer the armor. You could kick back and do the advising thing. You drink, I'll drive?"

"You were the one worried it might be able to identify my tactics."

"I did say that, didn't I?"

Like a grumpy father focused on the evening news, Kade was again absorbed by his holograms. N'Tomo, waiting for one of her own simulations to run, couldn't help but speak up.

"May I make a suggestion?"

Stark grinned fliratiously. "Always, Dr. N'Tomo."

Rolling her eyes, she walked over and pointed at the controls in Rogers's hands. "You're conditioned to respond to the environment with your entire body. But now, your actions are reduced to hand and finger movements. If you could find something analogous in your experience, like…"

He perked up. "My shield."

N'Tomo nodded. "Exactly. I've seen how you use it. It's like an extension of your body—you, but not you. Think of the armor as your shield."

"Great idea," Stark said. "But you're not going to throw the controller, right?"

"Tony, please," Rogers said. "I know what she means."

Cap tried again. The head of the armor tilted down. The rest of the figure curled after it, following an even arc, like a cross between a diver and a yogi. Soon, he had it headed roughly back toward the Helicarrier.

Stark nodded both his approval and relief. "Good. Not perfect, but good. Now, as long as you're up here, cut loose and bust a move."

"Bust a move?"

"Yeah. Run a combat maneuver, something that seems impossible, like moonwalking, but you can make it look easy, because you're Captain America."

There was a pause as they looked at each other. Stark blinked first. "Okay, forget impossible. Gimme like a barrel roll or a somersault."

Rogers thought of hurling his shield, making it sail through the air like his own fist. Trying to think of the suit the same way, he imagined the cloud cover as a gym floor he was standing on himself as he manipulated the controls. The suit did a half turn and flipped twice. For a moment, he felt a connection, but it vanished, and the suit awkwardly folded itself at the waist.

Stark made a face, then gave him a vague half-smile. "Close enough."

THE DARK path the sphere left through French wine country was easy to follow. It ended at the edge of a vineyard. There, every 15 minutes, the peace of the lush countryside was shattered by the Sleeper's recorded threat.

"Wenn Kapitän Amerika ist nicht hier innerhalb einer stunde, werden viele zivilisten sterben."

Still feeling the distance between himself and the armor, Rogers landed it about 50 yards away. Nia's suggestion worked in principle, but this was very different from using his shield. Rather than try to manipulate each limb, he activated an automated walking routine. Hoping the combination of his voice and Stark's electronic mimicry would trigger the identification, he approached the sphere.

"Looking for me?"

It wobbled.

Each tremor was accompanied by a series of clockwork clicks—heavier than the sound of the triangles, but not as loud. Using the suit's scanners, Cap studied the magnetic resonance image that appeared on the controller's small screen. Stark was right about his player-piano analogy. An open area in the orb's center was surrounded by a dense collection of gears, torsion springs, and ratchets. The mechanism was more appropriate to the Victorian era than World War II. They meshed, clacked, and whirred like a machine in a vintage penny arcade responding to the drop of a coin.

And then they stopped.

Rogers was about to announce himself again when the sphere shot forward. In an instant, it slammed into the armor, rolling it into the ground. Then it sat there, kneading the suit into the soft earth, clicking all the while.

It all happened so fast, Rogers doubted even Stark would have been able to get out of the way.

Tony seemed to agree. "The readings didn't show any acceleration.

It went straight from resting to 55 kilometers an hour, like it warped or something. Steve, get out of there."

"Thought you were just going to watch."

"I always talk during movies. Bad habit. But right now you're making my kick-ass armor look like that ingénue in the slasher movie who heads into the basement alone, and I'm telling you, get her out of there."

Taking the hint, Rogers pushed the throttle. The repulsor jets shot from the boots, but only created a spray of dirt. Realizing his mistake, he twisted the heels down. Finding the needed resistance, the armor began to press up and out.

Somehow, the sphere pushed back.

Was it making itself *heavier*?

Mindful of the sensitive lever, he moved it slowly to increase the thrust. When the sphere compensated, he popped it to the halfway mark.

In a blur of flying earth and rocks, the suit tore free. Before Stark could admonish him, Cap let go of the lever, allowing the autopilot to stabilize him in the air. The sphere dropped into the hole he'd left behind.

It didn't move at all until he landed. Then, once again, it tore toward him. Ready this time, he darted to the left. He nearly made it, but a loud clang filled his ears. The sphere had hit the armor's right boot. Warning messages flashed across the control screen. The boot had been dented.

"It's okay," Tony said. "I've got it insured. I think. Y'know, I'm just going to have a spare suit send itself our way so I can... Oh— look out!"

This time, Rogers avoided it completely. When the sphere came at the suit yet again, he recognized the pattern of clicks and whirrs it made before it moved, and only had to twitch himself out of the way like a hummingbird. After dodging a fourth and fifth time, he realized that like the first Sleeper, it was caught in a programming loop.

"We're closer to the English Channel than the Atlantic. Maybe I can lead it there."

"Take it slow. You saw what happened when it lost track of the Helicarrier," Fury said. "I'll try to establish a corridor along the shortest route."

The optimistic plan didn't last. After a few hundred yards, the sphere came too close for comfort again, raking his heel.

"Steve, you're thinking in two dimensions. Remember, you can also move up."

Tony's advice was good, but something else was going on. Had he mistimed his reaction, or was the Sleeper learning?

"I'm going to increase speed to—"

The final word never came out of his mouth. Without any clicks at all, the sphere bolted at the armor—and hit. Once again, it pressed the suit hard into the ground. Cap raised the thrusters to the halfway mark, but the sphere vibrated and held it in place.

The clanking mechanism inside it grew louder and faster. The gray surface lightened, then reddened with heat. More warning messages flashed on the HUD, tracking the rapidly rising temperature.

Rogers raised the thrust to 80 percent, but the sphere, smoldering now, was not letting the armor go. The heating technique reminded him of a different battle, one that had taken place years ago, against what he thought a more intelligent machine.

"The fourth Sleeper generated heat bursts, like a volcano."

"I'm getting its schematics from the S.H.I.E.L.D. archives now," Stark said. "Oh, yeah, some of the components match. Our new friend looks like an earlier effort. I don't think it's capable of volcanic temps, but it's still not something you want to be around when it blows."

Rogers pressed the lever all the way.

With a horrid scraping, the armor tore free. At the same moment, a wave of impossible heat burst from the orb. The air didn't burn, but everything else did: Vines, fencing, and earth all turned to ash. Their monitors were reduced to blocky static; the sound from the speakers became a vague crackling. Rogers let go of the thrust, but had no way of knowing whether the autopilot still worked.

Long, deathly silent moments passed before the armor's cameras came back online. It was hovering about 100 yards above the Sleeper, the suit's surface clouded by a stream of coolant hissing along the armor's surface. The sphere, not quite yet cool, was at the center of a flaming circle that stretched over a mile. In the distance, he saw blackened, smoking vehicles and several burning homes. He prayed they'd all been empty.

His mind had yet to take it all in before the dictator again spoke from beyond the grave:

"Sie sind nicht Kapitän Amerika."

You are not Captain America.

Tony voiced what he'd already guessed. "It's on to us. The blast fried the circuitry broadcasting your biometrics. We've got to do something before it engages a new routine."

"Blast it?"

"Not right now. The beam weaponry was damaged, too. I can re-route the power, but it'll take me a minute. See if you can keep it busy."

"Okay. We know it's hollow—let's see if it can crack."

"Uh, not exactly what I meant..."

Rogers pushed the thrusters to the max. As the suit careened toward the Sleeper, he wished it really *was* his shield. The sound it always made when it struck told him a lot about his foes. What the shield conveyed was wordless, informing not his mind, but his whole body, his muscle memory, allowing him to forge himself into a better weapon for the next strike.

The bright flash on the screen at the moment of impact gave him nothing. The suit's camera continued functioning, but it only showed a swirling blur. He had to look to the monitor array and single out a drone's distant feed to get even a slight sense of what had happened. There, he saw that Stark's pride and joy, the cutting edge of the cutting edge, had bounced off the smooth, featureless sphere like a dented ping-pong ball.

At least he'd remembered to let go of the thrust lever.

The armor, leaving a long trail of puffy white smoke, nearly left the drone's visual range before slowing. As it did, a piece tumbled from it like a bit of wreckage from a failed rocket. As the suit's camera steadied, he trained it on the debris.

It was an arm. He'd broken it. He'd broken the suit.

Stark took it in stride, or seemed to. "I'd make a joke about you costing me an arm and a leg, but I'm too busy stabilizing what's left to... Hold on. Crap! The Sleeper's up to something new."

Rogers snapped the armor's head back to the ground. The orb

was spinning. Far different from its lightning-quick strikes, this rotation started slowly, like a massive turbine moaning to life. Faster and faster it went, until it looked as if the centrifugal force might hurl it apart. All the while, it stayed in place, not kicking up so much as a clump of earth—as if the ground beneath it were air.

"Tony, any idea what's it doing?"

"All that running in place could be converting one form of energy to another, maybe to power up for another heat blast, or..."

As Stark spoke, it moved again, advancing beyond the parched land toward a steep hill. Beyond it lay a rural village smaller than the perimeter of the last heat blast.

Rogers tensed. "It must have detected the civilians. It's going for the town!"

"I'll get the weapons back online. You get in close enough, and we can fry the sucker."

Rogers sent the armor after the Sleeper. He cut it off easily and activated the targeting. The sundered arm joined in, zipping through the air to add its firepower.

The crack of the electric bolt was so sharp and deep, Rogers swore he felt it in his chest. Ionized by the discharge, the air between the suit and the Sleeper became a darker blue. The beam warped around the spinning surface, briefly covering it in a writhing second skin—and then the sphere absorbed it.

Rather than slow its advance, the attack had sped it up.

As it turned out, they didn't have to worry about the citizens. When the sphere reached the crest of the hill, it passed straight into the air.

Even Stark was so stunned all he could do was state the obvious.

"And now, well…it's flying. Yep. It's flying. It was never headed for the town. It's headed for us."

14

In the end, what's worth more—me, or the things that make me feel alive?

LAB 247 shuddered as the three sixth-generation fighter jets scrambled from the Helicarrier airstrip. Graceful as eagles—but four times faster—they sped toward their target.

Rogers maxed the thrust, but the armor lagged behind, its batteries recharging from the electric blast. Again, he wished he were out there facing the enemy head-on. The closer the sphere got, the more the safety of his quarantine chamber became an illusion, anyway.

But that kind of thinking was nothing more than a distraction. He had to focus on what he *could* do.

The armor began catching up, but not because it was going any faster. The Sleeper was slowing down. When the jet bays opened and deployed their missiles, it slowed even more.

Almost as if it was waiting for them.

"Nick, tell the jets to back off. Now!"

Fury didn't ask why—he simply relayed the command.

Two of the jets were already veering off when the sky filled with the light of a second sun. The heat wave hit the approaching missiles first. Their premature explosions rattled the jets. The pilots who were already turning rode out the concussive wave, skimming it as if surfing. The third pilot was not so lucky. The explosions hit head-on, scorching the fuselage and sending his craft into a spin. Recognizing engine failure, he ejected.

Seeing the pilot's chute billow, Rogers was briefly relieved—until the fabric fluttered in the heat and burst into flames.

Rogers aimed the armor toward the falling pilot. As he neared, readouts warned that the suit's metal surface was hot enough to sear flesh. Rather than grab the pilot, he snagged the paracords. They smoldered, but held. Tearing the burning chute free, he carried the airman to the Helicarrier deck.

He wasn't sure whether he'd saved the pilot or merely condemned him to a different kind of death. No longer hindered by the jets, the Sleeper sped toward them. As soon as it was close enough for the Helicarrier's forward guns to engage, the four 70mm electric cannons fired 200 rounds per second. All of them glanced off the sphere's surface.

The Sleeper's trajectory made it clear where it was headed—the hull just outside the lab.

"Tony, please tell me you've figured out how it's flying."

Out of ideas, Stark stood and slapped his thighs. "If I did, all due respect, I'd stop studying these readings and ask for my armor back. Best guess is electrogravitics, an electrical effect discovered by Thomas Townsend Brown in the 1920s. It relies on a corona discharge to produce an ionic wind that can transfer its momentum to surrounding neutral particles—"

The orb's impact seconds away, Steve cut him off. "Anti-gravity?"

"Yeah, okay, anti-gravity. But really, *you* could have said that."

"How do we stop it?"

"There are drill bits in the armor's fingertips tipped with boron nitride, harder than diamond," Stark said, scrambling. "They *might* be able to dig into the sphere and mess with its innards, but not while it's rotating like that. It'd take a million-to-one shot for the armor to latch on, let alone hold on long enough for the drills to get deep enough to—"

The sphere hit. The Helicarrier lurched sideways, and Stark, Rogers, and most of the crew were hurled off their feet. As the great ship listed, a horrible crunching erupted from beyond the hull.

It was trying to get inside.

First back on his feet, Fury screamed, "We've got a triple hull with a 5-inch hardened alloy, a 12-inch layer of high-speed fragment suppressor after that, and then *another* layer of hardened armor. Are you telling me that thing can get through all that?"

Stark pulled himself up next. "Not saying it can." The lights flickered. "Not saying it can't."

Lifting a bruised Kade, Nia called out. "Steve?"

"I'm fine." The controller in his hands, it didn't matter where he was, so he'd stayed on the floor. He maneuvered the armor through a sideways rain of projectiles. The suit's camera showed the spinning Sleeper ahead, digging wildly into the hull. Most of the debris generated by its efforts was shattered by the Helicarrier's cannon fire, while the sphere itself remained unharmed.

The fingers on the armor's remaining hand grew sharp. Their tips spun and whined, telling Rogers that Stark had activated the drill bits. The onboard computer offered a series of tactical suggestions, many contradictory. He ignored them, preferring to rely on the tentative feel he'd developed for the armor. He accelerated as he approached, trying to match the speed of the sphere's rotation. At the last instant, he curved the suit along the top of the stony blur and caught hold.

The suit gripped the surface by its one hand; the whirring fingertips dug in. As the armor was carried round and round, it enlarged the hole in the Helicarrier that the Sleeper was making. The rest of the view was a useless blur, but an extrapolated 3D image told Cap he'd managed to hang on for 436 rotations before the armor went flying off.

Inside the lab, the flickering lights died. The vibrations increased. The sphere was getting through.

Fury drew his sidearm and aimed it at the shaking wall. "I'll be damned if some crap Nazi tech is going to bring down my 21st-century Helicarrier!"

Matching his intensity, Rogers shouted back. "Nick, there's no contest! It wants me. Get everyone else out of here, now!"

Fury snarled, but then slipped the gun back into his holster. "You heard the man."

Glancing through the glass, Rogers saw him herd the others toward the door.

Kade staggered along, muttering. "If the heat blast destroys the virus, at least our problem will be solved."

Steve doubted the doctor cared whether he was heard or not. Seeing N'Tomo's reluctance to leave, he nodded her on. Stark refused to budge until Fury actually shoved the billionaire. "I'll be back. My auxiliary suit will be here in 60 seconds. The gloves don't have the same drill bits, but..."

He stopped short. Gloves. Plural. Both Rogers and Stark had the idea at the same time, but Cap said it first. "The arm. It's smaller than the whole suit. It would have a lot less trouble hanging on while it drills."

As Fury continued pushing him into the corridor, Stark hit some buttons. "Yes! The arm! Use the arm! I'm un-synching it from the rest of the suit!"

The door closed. Lit only by flashing red emergency lights, Cap sat with his back to the glass, refusing to look over his shoulder as the tearing and creaking grew louder. His focus had to be on the controls.

The arm had been keeping pace with the rest of the body. Now it flew free. It was also much easier to maneuver than the whole suit.

Bits of fragmented metal sprayed the glass. The Sleeper had breached the hull. If it was a little smaller, it would have gotten to him already. Its 15-foot diameter forced it to eat through both ceiling and floor to reach the quarantine chamber.

Zeroing in on the controls, Cap tried to hook the arm into the side of the sphere that was still spinning in the open air. The first time, it bounced off—but the second time, it grabbed hold. Unlike the larger suit, the arm was able to cling to the surface as it whipped around and around.

The drill bits were working, boring five holes into the strange material, but the arm lacked the power of the whole, slowing their progress. As the sphere tore through the lab, the holes deepened. In a game of inches, each edged closer to its goal.

If the sphere breached the isolation glass, Rogers figured he'd have to try to get around it. Maybe he could head for the hole it left behind, lead it away. Thousands of feet up, he might be able to get the suit to catch him—but he would not, under any circumstances, further endanger the Helicarrier crew.

The finger holes widened and became one. The metal hand disappeared inside the sphere. He thought it might actually work... until the edge of the sphere touched the glass.

Then, Cap briefly wondered what that date with Nia would have been like.

But the sphere stopped.

A gentle smoke trail twirled from the hole left by the burrowing glove. The concave shape gouged in the glass told him how close the Sleeper had come. The wall seemed intact, but when he held his bare fingers up to it, he felt the coolness of the outside air.

15

If I try to be objective, it's like trying to pick one snowflake over another.

ONCE the remotely operated hydraulic lifters removed the second Sleeper, Dr. Kade insisted on resealing the chamber himself. His hazmat suit making the process cumbersome, he struggled to position the heavy vacuum seal over the indentation. Rogers could only watch.

Once the suction disk was in place, Kade straightened. "This is temporary. With hull integrity compromised, we have to move you." In a rare show of sympathy, he added, "I'm afraid the secondary containment area will be less comfortable."

Rogers raised an eyebrow. "Is there a window?"

Kade shrugged. "One. And it's a bit smaller. There's something else I want to talk to you about."

"Of course. I admit I don't know a lot about your career, doctor, but Nia told me that you prevented an Ebola outbreak on your own. That's impressive work, and I'm sure you faced some tough choices."

"Thank you." Kade's face twitched, as if he were briefly struggling with the memory. In a way, it made the gaunt, fragile figure remind Rogers of himself before the Super-Soldier serum. Whatever Kade was feeling, he quickly put it aside. "That exactly the sort of situation I came to discuss. I've seen many hot-zone workers expose themselves to lethal diseases to comfort patients who are already dying and contagious. That strikes me as callous. If the workers sicken, they won't be able to help others who could be saved. Yet when they surrender to this base communal instinct, something that even canines have, they're called *brave*. Do you think those same instincts motivate you?"

Rogers frowned. They were more different than he realized. "If providing comfort to the dying means acting like a dog, maybe you underestimate dogs. Me, I've spent my life following the soldier's creed, *nemo resideo*: leave no one behind. Risking my life on behalf of people otherwise considered lost may seem callous to you, but there'd be a lot of men and women dead right now if I hadn't done just that. *Any* time I risk my life, I suppose I create the possibility I won't be able to save anyone else in the future, but it comes with the territory."

Not satisfied, Kade tried to explain further. "Let me give you a hypothetical. A train carrying 100 adults is headed for a cliff. You can activate a switch to change its course and save them. If you do, though, the train will kill a single child standing on the other track. Do you save the 100 adults or the single child?"

"I'd try to save both."

He shook his head. "You can't. You have to decide, don't you see? You're the one carrying the virus. When it comes down to it, you are the one responsible. How much I can trust you to make the right decisions is crucial to making my own."

Rogers tried. "Who are the 100 adults? Is the child Adolf Hitler? Is Jonas Salk or Martin Luther King Jr. on the train? What magic prevents me from trying to save them all? I'm not trying to be flip about your concerns, I get the need, but hypotheticals are abstract. Life happens in specifics. Even if I did answer, I doubt it would truly give you what you're looking for. Having been in so many real situations, that's not a decision I could make outside of the moment. I didn't know my father long, but one thing he told me stuck: Talk is cheap. Don't listen to what I say, watch what I do. That's the best I can give you, doc."

Kane pursed his lips. "Fair enough. If you'll excuse me, I'd like to get out of this suit."

Before he exited, Rogers called to him. "Dr. Kade? What would you do—save the child or the adults?"

"The adults, of course."

Rogers nodded. "Of course."

An hour later, the door opened again. He worried Kade was back to ask if a tree fell in a forest and no one was there to hear it, would it make a sound. But it was Fury.

"I know you've been in blackout with the area network down, but I couldn't send anyone in until the integrity of the chamber seal was secure. I assume Kade gave you the news?"

"No. What news?"

"The signal from the sphere wasn't about echolocation. It was transmitting. We thought it was as a steady tone, until Velez, one of our Signals Intelligence agents, realized it was a condensed version of Morse code. It was sending data."

"Then there'll be more."

ONCE again, the castle's quiet was interrupted by the Sonikey's high-pitched shriek. This time it didn't make Schmidt feel like trying to rip his own head apart. Zola considered this to be a good sign.

"The palliative drugs I gave you have provided some relief?"

The Skull picked up the humming crystal and twirled it between steady fingers. "Perhaps. But they do say laughter is the best medicine. Seeing my 'noble' foe forced to fight by proxy provided some much-needed *schadenfreude*."

He smiled at the reporters and pundits filling the screens, all questioning why Captain America had not battled the sphere himself.

"It hurt for him not to be there. I know it. It made him feel powerless, as impotent as an insect that can only dream of being a man. I hope he found it…humiliating."

Zola pointed to the humming device. "The next Sleeper—can you guess where it is? What it might look like?"

The Skull shrugged. "No, but I'm confident we'll find out shortly. If the first two were any indication, I trust it will not disappoint."

If I were as callous as the stars, I'd flip a coin. But that would be the same as not deciding at all.

EVERYTHING in Dede Clayton's field of vision was boring: the dark room, the murky underwater images on her insanely expensive monitor, even the incessant droning that dribbled artlessly from her $20,000 speakers.

"Once the Japanese decimated the U.S. fleet at Pearl Harbor, the crucial oil shipments in the Gulf of Mexico were easily within reach of the new Nazi subs."

Once, Dede had been a well-paid oceanographer, but worsening asthma forced her to abandon the heady rush of deep-sea diving. Now she was stuck at home, logging shots as they streamed live from a Remotely Operated Vehicle hundreds of miles away, and some 5,000 feet below, off Florida's western coast.

It wasn't unusual to log on the fly like this, but listening to a guide track was certainly different. The deadline was so tight, a teen PA on the ship had recorded the rough narrative to give her the sense of the timing they wanted.

"On July 30, 1942, 45 miles east of the Mississippi delta, the S.S.

Robert E. Lee was attacked by *U-166*. A single torpedo sunk the ship in about 15 minutes, killing 25."

Mostly, she found it a distraction. The PA could barely pronounce the words. It would all be changed anyway when their has-been actor dubbed the final version before the special aired next week.

But it wasn't her decision.

Snapping the pull tab on another diet soda, she briefly debated pouring it into her computer. She could tell the producers she'd had some unexpected equipment failure. Too bad she needed the money, even though the gig only paid half her old rate.

"Naval patrol boat *PC-586* spotted the periscope and dropped 10 depth charges. The oil slick that surfaced told them what happened to the sub."

At least the ROV operators could give her something decent to look at. They were paying for her expert eye, but hadn't even provided a high-res feed. All she could see was murky water occasionally interrupted by vague geometric shapes covered in crud.

"It wasn't until an archeological survey in 2001 that this wreckage was actually discovered."

As the voice droned on, she thought: *Is that freaking shadow supposed to be the sub? Dear Lord, I hope the real thing looks better. Maybe I should have them keep my name off this.*

Finally, the camera showed a ragged 10-foot hole in the hull.

The guide track continued. "Is this the breach that spelled the U-boat's doom?"

The ROV pivoted, trying for a peek inside. But the operator—as if driving a rental car instead of a delicate instrument subject to ocean currents—failed to compensate for the drift. The million-dollar piece of equipment that comprised most of their budget hit the edge of the hole.

The image shook and briefly filled with static.

Amateurs, she thought. *Newcomers. Idiots. Wait...*

The picture cleared. At first, Dede thought the ROV lights were bouncing off the old sub's interior, but the dull red glow wasn't a reflection—it was a source. Something inside the wreck was giving off light.

Her eyesight was perfect, but she squinted at the screen. "Now there's something you don't see every day."

The light grew—or rather, its source came closer to the lens. It was probably a big fish. Bioluminescence was common among deep-sea creatures. With any luck, they'd stumbled on an interesting cephalopod.

The view briefly returned to the green-gray water, then steadied on the breach. At least the ROV operator had the sense to back up and get out of its way.

None of the animals she knew were cube-shaped. Was it another ROV they neglected to mention? There was a sphere-shaped hollow in the center. Something to bring up samples?

Whatever it was, it was trying to get out. Poorly positioned to clear the uneven breach, the cube hit the ragged, rusty edge. As it tipped out, its details grew clearer, or as clear as the crappy feed allowed. Its color somewhere between silver and brass, it looked new, unlike the wreck's rotting steel.

There was a triangular indentation on what she assumed was its top. But a cube didn't necessarily have a top, did it? That could be its side, or even bottom.

There was a red flash, and the screen went blank. The dreadful narration stopped. She tried the microphone. Excited for the first time in two years, she had to think a moment to remember the production assistant's name.

"Dale? What's going on?"

Nothing.

The backup Skype line to the salvage ship beeped. Dede nearly broke her mouse clicking the answer button, but no video appeared. The app explained that only audio could be provided. It didn't say why.

The sound of screams and rushing water emerged from her hybrid electrostatic speakers, their highs and lows flattened by limited bandwidth. Even so, the poor quality of the recorded voice she heard next was obvious. If the words hadn't been dominating the news for the last 48 hours, Dede never would have made them out:

"Wo ist Kapitän Amerika?"

Then came a horrible crunching, as if the whole ship was collapsing as easily as the aluminum can in her hand.

Despite Dede Clayton's love of the wide sea and its many, miraculous mysteries, she felt lucky to be stuck at home.

KADE hadn't exaggerated about the size of the auxiliary iso-chamber. If Rogers didn't know he was a patient, he'd think he was being subjected to psychological torture. The close gray-metal walls made him feel like he was inside a toaster. Worse, the view from the one-foot-square window consisted of a featureless room and a door. Even the panel by the window that monitored his vitals was frustratingly outside his field of vision.

The *isolation* part of isolation chamber was sinking in. Nia and

Kade were in another lab. Fury was at the helm. Stark was in the cargo bay, trying to ensure that the wrecked Sleepers weren't still transmitting somehow. Putting on a brave face for himself seemed pointless.

Rogers breathed into his growing discomfort as best he could, but still grimaced at the two-inch video feeds on Kade's laptop that showed the third Sleeper's progress. Thank heavens Agent Velez in Signals was earning her keep. She'd snagged the distress call, traced an Internet connection to its West Coast Florida address, and uncovered a frantic 9-1-1 call from a freelance video editor.

As a result, by the time the Sleeper came ashore on Captiva Island, a wide safety zone had been evacuated. That proved critical: Unlike the others, the cube didn't withhold its attacks. Since making landfall, red beams—some form of proto-laser—shot from its four corners, obliterating anything in its path. On the island, that only meant a beach and a golf course—but it was headed staight for Cape Coral, population 200,000.

The city wasn't its target. So far, it was only asking for Rogers' location, like the triangles. Stark insisted it was out of range for whatever data the sphere had broadcast. But how long before it switched tactics and started threatening lives?

And he was stuck in here.

A little image of Fury popped up on the screen, reminding Rogers that he wasn't as alone as he thought. "Look at the bright side."

"What bright side? Those hollows match the size and shape of the other Sleepers. I don't need an engineer to tell me they're designed to combine, just like the first three I tangled with."

"Yeah, but we did need engineers to confirm that whatever they were intended to do, the triangles and the sphere are nothing more than junk now. Even Stark's confirmed that it'd take something with the power of the Cosmic Cube to put them back together. And the fact that this one only has space for two others means this could be the last of them."

"'Could,' Nick. 'Could.'"

"You got better, I'm all ears." Fury's face disappeared.

As he watched the Sleeper's progress, Steve Rogers felt… What? Drone pilots experienced a bodiless sensation as they stared at their satellite views. If anything, he felt the opposite. Even in the early days when he was physically weaker, he could still attack a threat directly. Knocked down, he could always try again. Now, his body ached to show it still existed.

His fingers gripped the laptop so tightly, it was about to shatter. Only Nia's appearance outside the small window saved it. Collecting himself, he set the computer aside and rose to greet her.

Her arm was bent at the elbow, as if she was carrying a coat, but there was nothing there. He started to make a quip about the emperor's new clothes, but then the near-transparent material she held folded in a way that caught the light.

"I hesitate to call this good news," she said, "but it counts as *better* news."

"'It' being?"

She held it closer for him to see. "A self-healing polymer that mimics certain properties of Vibranium. It was created in a Wakandan research facility. There are currently only three prototypes. Until recently they were kept under the tightest security my country can provide.

"So it's…stolen?"

She raised her eyebrows and tilted her head. "Here we enter a gray area. Given the worldwide need, unless and until the process is perfected, T'Challa would rather its origin remain secret. So this membrane doesn't exist, and you didn't hear me say any of that."

Rogers scrunched his face. "Sounds like quite a breakthrough."

Folding it carefully, she placed it in the secure-transfer drawer. "It is. The membrane is thin enough so you can wear your uniform over it, but it will cover you completely—mouth, eyes, ears. It will filter your exhalations and even reseal over minor wounds, including cuts and gunshots. The only thing you won't be able to do in it is relieve yourself."

"No bathroom breaks, then." Opening his side of the drawer, he pressed the fabric between his fingers. It felt like…nothing. "Even this wouldn't convince Kade that I should be in combat again, especially after last time."

She shook her head. "Seeing how the Sleeper ripped through the Helicarrier made Dr. Kade very much aware of the extent of the current threat. If something like that happened again, he knows you'd have to fight. But…he has other reasons for agreeing to a new protocol."

He looked up. "Such as?"

She turned to the right, toward the screen displaying his vitals. "How are you holding up?"

Brow furrowed, he smiled, wondering where this was headed. "Well, doctor, I'm not going to say it's been easy."

"I wouldn't believe you if you did." After scanning a moment, she blinked. "Your blood pressure's up a little. Normally I'd say it's nothing, but your vitals are known to be rock steady. According to the files, your heart rate is as reliable as the atomic clock in Switzerland."

"I'll keep that in mind if I'm ever looking for a new job. Are you worried it's an effect of the virus?"

She eyed the tiny chamber and pursed her lips. "My guess is it's environmental. But let's see. I'd like to tell you a story that might help. I was in West Africa, part of a team working in the hot spots during an Ebola outbreak. In one of the stricken villages, I would often help a young teacher. She had the money to flee, but refused to abandon her students. With so many dying, the children often asked why there was no way to help, no cure. She felt obligated to prepare their young minds for the fact that sometimes there is *nothing* you can do. So she asked the class a question, 'What would you do if a lion was chasing you?' One boy, Amad, shot his hand up. 'I will climb a tree,' he said. The teacher said, 'Good, but what if the lion also climbs the tree?' 'I will jump in the river and swim,' he answered. 'And if the lion also jumps in the water and swims?' When he hesitated, she thought she was getting the idea across, but he made a face and said, 'Teacher, are you on my side or the lion's?'"

When Steve laughed, Nia checked his vitals again. "Ah, you see? I was right. Your blood pressure dropped back to normal. I have a great bedside manner."

"No disagreement," he said. "But I'm still waiting for the other shoe to drop. Dr. Kade? New protocols?"

"He's agreed to allow your release under certain extreme situations because of some...decisions that have been made."

"Decisions?"

Before she could answer, Fury's voice squawked from the laptop again. "Got some more good news. The second Sleeper only realized it'd been duped when that heat blast knocked out the biometric transmission from the Iron Man suit, right? Well, since this third one apparently can't detect your baby-blues from all the way overseas, we started power-broadcasting your biometrics, and it's taking the bait. We're steering it, even from way over here."

"Great! Where are we taking it?"

There was an odd pause. "I figured Dr. N'Tomo would've told you that by now. She's there, right?"

Rogers eyed her. "Yep. She was just about to get to that, but why don't you fill me in?"

"Okay. We're trying to lead it to the most isolated place there is from sea to shining sea—the Big Empty in southeast Oregon, 24,000 square miles of high desert. If it follows us, and we can't neutralize it, you and that fancy membrane can have a go with no one around for hundreds of miles."

He kept looking at Nia. "What am I not getting?"

She shrugged. "Reaching the high desert isn't only about isolating the Sleeper—it's about isolating you."

Fury piped in. "With the biggest property owner being the government, it's no surprise S.H.I.E.L.D.'s got a base up there. More an old warehouse, really, but it'll…uh…suit our purposes. Once the Sleeper threat is nullified, it's where you'll be placed in cryogenic suspension."

Cap blinked and rubbed his temples. "I'd almost forgotten. So what is this, Nick, my last hurrah?"

The colonel bristled. "Don't be stupid. It doesn't suit you. Once this Sleeper business blows over, we'll lick this thing. Stark's freeing up some new quantum computers that'll drop the calculation time by a factor of 10, and we've got Richards, Xavier, and Banner on tap to…"

Fury's voice seemed to fade as Rogers realized how soon he would be yanked from the world again, frozen. From the beginning, reporters, admirers, friends, and acquaintances—seeing him in action, thinking him brave—would ask how he did it. His answer was always the same. *I just do.*

So when he wondered how others somehow managed to go to their deaths in peace and dignity, he imagined them answering: *I just did.*

"...with that crowd on it, you know they'll..." Finally noticing Rogers' silence, Fury flinched. "I'm...I'm gonna give you a minute."

"I don't need a minute."

"Then I'm gonna give me a minute." He clicked off.

His gaze drifted over to Nia. She was scanning his vitals again, this time looking worried.

"Blood pressure up again?"

Even her slight smile brought some warmth to the room. "Not so most would notice. I wish I had another joke for you, but I'm not sure it would help." She put her hand up to the window. "We haven't known each other long, but if you'd care to share what you're feeling, I'd be honored."

He wanted to take her up on the offer, but wasn't sure how. "I'm no stranger to inevitability, Nia. I'll do what I have to, accept what I have to, but..."

"Yes?"

"Well, I'm with Amad. If the lion followed me into the water, I'd dive and swim faster."

"No, you wouldn't," she said. "You'd turn and face the lion."

It can't just be luck that decides for me, it has to be the pattern. The design.

WE HIT that tailwind yet?"

With the formidable director of S.H.I.E.L.D. standing uncomfortably close, Helmsman Escalon turned to answer. "Yes, sir. The thrusters compensated to maintain velocity."

"Eyes on your station!" Fury snapped.

"Yes, sir."

Rogers' voice sounded in his earbud. "A little harsh, Nick?"

Fury huffed. "The only surprise we've had the last few hours is the lack of surprises, and I don't want anyone gettin' complacent. Me, I'm antsy enough cruising this low and this slow, but I gotta admit, Stark's projections are working perfectly."

"Don't tell him that."

"Don't have to. He already knows. After the first two hours, he took off to leave the boring stuff for us lesser minds."

"Where to?"

"Eh, collecting some equipment for the base."

Fury knew Rogers too well not to be able to see behind the

mask, and he could tell the situation had begun to wear on the man. He decided not to mention that Stark was assembling his own team to work on the virus. Rogers would probably think Stark should stay focused on the Sleepers until that threat was resolved.

They were traveling steadily over the deserts of New Mexico at an altitude close enough to keep the third Sleeper on their tail, but far enough to stay out of its weapons' range. Apparently unable to fly, it dogged them on the ground, moving at a steady pace, firing its high-density energy beams only to remove obstacles—and occasionally telling Steve in German that he should prepare to die. There were four guns, each swivel-mounted on its corners. Otherwise, its streamlined appearance—a cube with a spherical hollow in the center—gave them little to go on.

"The Helicarrier can maintain a constant velocity in all sorts of meteorological conditions," Fury continued. "So unless a Category 5 hurricane appears out of nowhere, it's steady as she goes for the next six hours. On the other hand, having seen Category 5 hurricanes appear out of nowhere, I'm sitting on my crew."

There was another reason Fury was being more curt than usual. He was trying to distract himself from the sick feeling in his gut over what they planned for his friend. Knowing the cryo-chamber was already in place at the Big Empty base didn't help.

"Run a complete systems check."

"Sir, we just did that five minutes ag—"

"If I wanted to know the time, I'd look at my wristwatch. Just do it!"

"Yes, sir."

Kade appeared on the bridge uninvited, his scarred face twisted in anger, his thin frame tensed and ready for a fight. At first, Fury was relieved to see someone he could feel good about arguing with. When the world-class expert gave him that arrogant sneer, he felt even better about it.

"You love your secrets, don't you?" Kade said.

The colonel sneered back at him. "We *are* spies, doc. We *protect* secrets. The Super-Soldier serum is one of our biggest, but I made sure you had access to everything we have on Cap, didn't I?"

Kade raised his eyebrows. "Except this. *This* I had to dig for."

He held up a PDA.

Seeing what was on it, Fury hissed. "Schmidt's files."

Kade's irate, reedy voice filled the helm. "But he's not exactly Johann Schmidt anymore, is he? Not biologically. His brain patterns were transferred into a clone of Steve Rogers. What a pity our best *spies* couldn't *protect* their biggest secret from their real enemies!"

When heads turned, Fury let his frustration show. "Unless this bridge is exploding, the next one to look back here will be cleaning the head with dental floss!"

He adjusted his black body suit and faced the doctor. "I'm not much on courtesy myself, doc, and I don't really care whether you respect me or not, but for the sake of keeping my crew focused while they're working to save lives, you *will* keep your voice down." Exhaling deep, he continued. "You're right. I screwed up. I should have had that sent to you with the rest. You're thinking it's possible the Skull also has the virus?"

"Not just *possible*! Given what I know about how the virus binds with DNA, it's as certain as the sunrise!"

Steve's voice sounded in Fury's ear. "That may explain why the

Sleepers are appearing now. If the Skull knows he has the virus, he could be trying for his last hurrah."

"I'm putting you on speaker so the doc here doesn't think I'm talking to myself. I already feel enough like an idiot." Fury rubbed his stubble. "If that's true, step one is finding him. The Sleepers can ID Cap's biometrics. Maybe we can figure out how to use them to track the Skull."

Kade's expression grew less dark, more thoughtful. "That could work. I could use some focused time alone, and I suspect Dr. N'Tomo could do without my company for a while. I'd like to have her oversee that process, assuming you'll grant her the appropriate clearance."

Fury responded to the barb with a quick nod. "Next question is what we do with him when we find him."

"Isn't it obvious? He must be neutralized, as quickly and efficiently as possible."

Fury grimaced. "You mean you want us to whack him?"

"Yes. Some form of incineration would be best. The temperature should exceed—"

The director's hand snapped up. "Let me stop you right there. Even if I don't have a problem with this in principle, it's not as if we've ever executed anyone because they're sick, even if we don't like them."

Kade's irritation turned to confusion. "But...the man's a war criminal. His activities during World War II alone would earn him the death penalty a dozen times. Under the circumstances, why make any effort to keep him alive?"

Rogers answered on speaker. "Because we're not murderers."

The doctor didn't skip a beat. "Call it an execution if it makes you feel better. It's beyond me why you'd want to follow the letter of the law now, when you seem so willing to bend it in less important situations. But I'm sure with the proper pressure, we could ask the international court to try him in absentia and..."

Steve cut him off. "You really *don't* understand, do you?"

Kade straightened. His stretched neck and lean body, coupled with his small bulging eyes, made him look like a meerkat. "All due respect, but I'm starting to think I'm the only one who *does* understand."

*If I had a million years, I could think through to certainty,
but I don't. I have to decide—and soon.*

HOURS before the media came to its garbled conclusions about the Helicarrier's low altitude and very visible path, S.H.I.E.L.D.'s strategy was obvious to the Skull, and it suited his purposes seamlessly. He was relieved, but to admit that meant he'd had doubts about his plan—and his survival. Rather than claim such a weakness, he projected the feeling, transforming it into an opportunity to assure his companion of his certainty.

"There, you see, Arnim? I was right."

The android concurred. "Yes. As you predicted, the Helicarrier is leading the final Sleeper to some remote location so Rogers can face it without risking the infection of others. At that point, what they mistakenly think of as wreckage will be in close quarters, awaiting final activation by the Sonikey."

Whatever feelings Schmidt kept hidden, he could not deny the rush he felt now. "Could things go more perfectly?"

"More perfectly is a redundancy. Perfection is an absolute state. Something is either perfect or it is not. Nothing can be *more* or *less* perfect."

Consumed by a sudden, giddy sense of strength, the Skull found it impossible to conceal his amusement. "Dr. Zola, I believe you've given new meaning to the term 'grammar Nazi.'"

Schmidt could practically hear the processors analyzing Zola's emotional response. Interpreting it as surprise, the avatar supplied an appropriately befuddled expression. "Did you just tell a joke?"

The Skull smirked. "Unusual, is it not?"

The avatar formed lines along its brow that showed concern. "It is singular. I shall double-check your last test results."

Another symptom, was it? The notion that Schmidt's confidence might be driven by a thoughtless virus was deeply offensive.

Or was even that an overly emotional reaction?

His exaggerated joy faded, and he found himself scrambling to explain.

"It's just that for the first time since you told me about the virus, I felt…"

"Undefeatable?"

Before he could agree, he went into another coughing fit, spewing dollops of blood onto his chin. They were coming more frequently now. A half minute later, it seemed to be over. The bits of clear saliva that mixed with the red were oddly easier to see. Before he could wipe his mouth, though, his eyes went wide with a new pain. His chest burned; his throat swelled as if he were being strangled.

He tumbled first into the desk, and then toward Zola. "Uhn…"

Android arms reached out to steady the Skull. For the first time, Schmidt accepted the assistance. He even allowed Zola to help him back into his chair. Then Zola moved away without comment.

In an even more surprising gesture, Schmidt tugged him back.

The Skull stared—not at the projected face, but at the camera lens, behind which he knew the geneticist's mind truly dwelled. "Arnim, how far would you go to stay alive? Have you ever imagined there might be a limit?"

"The best predictor of future behavior is past behavior. You well know that I could have transferred my brain patterns into a human host like yours. Instead I chose a much more durable form, so that I might better—in your words—stay alive. If there is a limit to this desire in me, I have yet to encounter it."

Satisfied, Schmidt let go. "In that we are the same." His fingers stiff from the effort of clutching Zola, he tugged off his leather gloves. "There is no crime, against the world or my own form, that I would hesitate to commit to maintain my existence." His head lowered. For a moment he wasn't sure whether he was staring into the fire on purpose, or too weak to move his neck. "All the same, I must confess that the pain I am experiencing is...unique."

"Unique," Zola repeated. "Unique in type or intensity?"

A familiar hum and click told him Zola was accessing his medical equipment, retrieving the most recent test results.

The Skull tightened what there was of his lips. "Both."

"You wouldn't be the first to believe in things worse than death."

This was Zola's version of small talk. The data must be taking longer than expected to analyze. Trusting he'd be given any new information as soon as it was available, the Skull saw no reason not to participate in the distraction.

"You misunderstand me. Death is not better or worse. It is nothing. Pain, on the other hand, can be inspiring."

"Then is it possible your increased pain has inspired you to understand why a lesser being might choose to end their own life rather than suffer?"

What was Zola on about? Did he still believe the plan might fail? Was he trying to prepare him for the end?

Schmidt grabbed the chair's arms, and ran his palms up and down their length. "Sympathy for the weak, no. A more abstract appreciation? Not even that. I am only surprised that I've yet to experience all the extremes this body has to offer." He squeezed the chair so tightly the veins on the back of his hands stood out. "Were I reduced to a quivering blob capable of only pain, my rage would sustain me until the last. Beyond the last."

Zola stepped back from his equipment. "That is fortunate for you. I've already explained how the virus cleverly travels along the nervous system rather than through the bloodstream, where antibodies might attack it. In one sense, while there will be these occasional fits, your vital organs will be the last to be attacked. In the meantime, though, the new tests confirm the pain will soon become far worse."

Worse?

The sensation of abject terror rose so powerfully, Schmidt couldn't keep it from his face. But in the next moment, he buried it—hard and deep. "I can't give up. Not when I'm so close."

"Understood. Yet even if the Sleepers assemble, there remains the question of your presence. May I ask how you plan to reach them?"

Despite the pinkish sweat dripping freely down his cheeks, the Skull managed a grin. He'd been given yet another opportunity to assure someone else of his certainty.

"*This* is your concern? Oh, doctor, that won't be a problem at all. Don't you see? They will bring me to it."

True beauty that can make the very idea of luck seem meaningless, a placeholder for a lack of understanding.

THE VASTNESS of the Oregon high desert was a stark contrast to the quarantine chamber—yet in their sterility, their emptiness, they still were somehow the same. As the drone hover-flier set Steve Rogers down in the Big Empty, the first line of Fats Waller's "Ain't Misbehavin'" ran through his head:

"No one to talk to, all by myself."

That was the idea, after all. No one to see, no one to hurt, no one to infect. Even the nearest cattle that somehow grazed on this barren land were over 100 miles away.

Despite the membrane that kept him from feeling the clean air against his skin or tasting it on his tongue, the sense of scale was humbling. Other than the heat, the flat nothing and overwhelming sky reminded him of the stretches of icy tundra that the Nazis faced during Operation Barbarossa, their attempted invasion of Russia. On a violent winning streak, they were unprepared for the landscape's constant reminder of how small they truly were. With 75 percent of their military committed to the invasion, they encountered complete defeat—physical and psychological—for the first time.

Such expanses drew a different reaction from him—a sensation that seemed alien to the arrogant Nazis—awe.

The decision to deploy him had come swiftly. They were still miles from the hidden base. But the cube, as if it had run out of patience, had halted and changed its announcement to the now-familiar death threat:

"Wenn Kapitän Amerika ist nicht hier innerhalb einer stunde, werden viele zivilisten sterben."

The likely explanation Stark phoned in from Silicon Valley was that only luck had gotten them this far. Rather than chase a signal forever, Tony reasoned it had to be on a timer, that it *should* have already moved on to its next routine—stopping and playing its recording—but age had frozen whatever mechanisms were responsible. The long journey must have shaken its pianola gears loose.

A low whistling wind made Fury's voice through the comm sound faint. "It's about two clicks east."

Rogers saw it. Far, far off, its square lines sparkled through the heat waves. But it was getting smaller, headed away from him. Not realizing how close he was, it was trying to find civilians to slaughter.

To get its attention, he hurled his shield, long and hard. Standing still, he watched the curved metallic shape sail off. It practically disappeared before a familiar, ringing *clunk* told him it had struck the cube. It bounced off, back toward him, but the momentum he usually relied on wouldn't be enough to carry it back across this distance.

Not a problem. The magnets in his shield and glove, activated by a press of his fingers into his palm, sent it singing back. The growing *whoosh* telling him exactly where the shield was in its return journey, he kept his eyes on the cube.

Did one hit do the trick, or would the Sleeper need more?

The cube stopped getting smaller—but still wasn't heading toward him. He thought he heard something from it, but the *thunk* of the shield slapping his glove briefly drowned it out. Then he heard it again: a low ticking. Remembering the sphere, he thought it might be the cube's inner gears meshing—but no, that wasn't it.

He was hearing the energy beams he'd seen on the video feeds. From the top four corners, they sliced the air and ground, making the cube look like a fat, square spider with thin, ruby-colored legs. Unlike legs, the beams didn't propel the cube, but they ticked as they turned.

Were they acting as sensors, trying to locate him?

A moment later, it again moved away from him. He threw the shield. This time, he followed at a brisk pace, dry sand rising with each step. When the shield returned, he prepared to throw it yet again without breaking his gait—but the cube finally reacted.

Like the bad guy in a classic Western duel, it pivoted in Cap's direction. Coming toward him now, its weapons fired in an angled, crisscross pattern. Seeing it on the monitors was one thing, but in person, Fury's hopeful conclusion seemed more certain. The spaces in the cube were clearly intended to house the other two Sleepers. They were meant to combine. The fact that there were only *two* such spaces in the cube that needed to be filled made it more likely that this *was* the last of them.

The only part he wasn't completely sure about was if the others had truly been destroyed. But if the Nazis had access to something like the Cosmic Cube, World War II would have been much different.

To match its deliberate pace, he slowed. The only sounds were

Cap's crunching boots and the sandy hiss of the sliding cube. As the distance closed, its message changed.

"Kapitän Amerika, endlich ihre schwäche wird von der ganzen welt gesehen warden!"

Captain America, at last your weakness will be revealed for all the world to see!

The expectation of victory further confirmed the likelihood this was the final Sleeper. Otherwise, any resonance Hitler's voice might've had fell flat against the wide terrain. The taunts seemed as old and meaningless as the whines of an antique talking doll.

"Kapitän Amerika, werden Sie schnell und suredly sterben wie jeder, der das ewige Reich zu widersetzen!"

Captain America, you will fall as quickly and assuredly as any who seek to oppose the Eternal Reich!

The word *eternal* was especially ironic. The Nazis believed there were three German reichs, or empires. The first, the Holy Roman Empire, lasted nearly a thousand years. The second, the monarchy that began with Germany's unification, survived forty-seven.

The third, the one Hitler proclaimed eternal, lasted only twelve.

No point in explaining that to a recording, though.

A ticking and a silvery glint of sunlight against metal told him the energy beams were realigning, aiming his way. The four red lines burned across the terrain, heating the sand they hit into a brittle, glass-like shell. The attack was so utterly telegraphed, he jumped easily out of the way.

Landing closer to the cube, he rose and took several more steps before it fired again.

He raised his shield to block, hoping to get a better sense of what he was up against. As the energy cascaded along the curved surface, he felt pressure and heat—but it wasn't hot enough to burn him through the shield, let alone harm the Vibranium. If Stark was right, and time had left it damaged, maybe its weapons were losing their charge.

With the next blast, though, the intensity increased a thousand-fold, hurling him off his feet.

He landed hard. The beams had been blocked by the shield, but his forearm vibrated, as if it had been exposed to a powerful electric current. The still-crackling shield too hot to hold, he was forced to let go. Wobbling against the ground, it hissed, louder and softer, depending on its angle to the sand.

The assault paused as the beams somehow met in midair. He moved. The cube unleashed a single, focused blast. This one didn't simply melt sand into glass—it gouged a two-foot hole where he'd been standing.

The ruby needles of the rays came at him, again crisscrossing the air, erasing any escape route. Hitting left and right, they advanced too quickly for him to dodge by moving backwards.

With only one direction left, he leapt forward. Unsure if he'd been fast enough, he arced his body to fit through the narrowing space between the beams. Ahead, he saw the sleek, square shape and its spherical hollow. From behind, he felt a stinging at his heel and caught a whiff of something burning.

When he landed, his heel stung, but not enough to slow him. The cube's swivel-mounts made the beam weapons perfect for covering a wide area at long or medium range—but now that he was nearer, he didn't see how they could fire at all without hitting the cube itself. Diving closer still, he scouted the spherical hollow for any other weakness he might exploit.

By the time he realized he'd done exactly what the cube—or rather, its designers—expected him to do, it was too late. With a terrible grinding, metal bands slapped out from the hollow's curve and tried to snare his arms and legs. He might have gotten out of their reach were it not for the firing beams blocking his retreat.

All he could manage was an odd dance, flailing his arms and legs this way and that to avoid the slapping bands. Before he could detect any pattern to their movements, one snagged the ankle above his wounded foot. Its edge curled around to meet itself, forming an unyielding brace. It twisted one way, then the other, trying to pull him off balance.

S.H.I.E.L.D. was watching from the Helicarrier. They had to be planning something by now. Rogers called into the comm, but the only response was digital static. The cube was scrambling communications, he realized.

He kept moving, but soon the slapping bands caught his left wrist, then his right. Struggling against them proved fruitless. The thing had been built to restrain him—of course his strength had been taken into account. Once he was firmly secured, the bands pulled back, centering him in the spherical hollow. The deadly beams withdrew. The cube clicked and whirred, this time exactly the same way the sphere had. The sounds repeated in an almost musical fashion.

Much as he trusted Fury, Cap wasn't about to stand by and wait to see what happened next.

It was designed to kill him. Figuring out how might be key to avoiding that fate. The usual methods were easy to imagine. The cube could contract, crushing him—or expand, ripping him apart. It might explode, or give off a heat blast similar to the sphere.

Given all the trouble Hitler gone through to build and hide these Sleepers, all that seemed too simple.

A grate opened above him, releasing a dry, white powder that tumbled over his body. His first thought was anthrax, but a tiny amount of that would do the job, and this powder kept coming.

Baking soda?

It didn't make sense. What was it up to? He scoured his memory of all it'd said, hoping to find some clue in the phrasing.

...prepare to meet your doom.

...at last your weakness will be revealed for all the world to see!

...you will fall as quickly and assuredly as any who seek to oppose the Eternal Reich!

Eternal. Right.

The Sleepers he'd originally faced were intended to destroy the world. They were built for use in the event that Germany *lost*. But if Tony was right, these had been created earlier, before the defeat at Operation Barbarossa, when a Nazi victory was considered the only possibility. The bravado behind the recordings, the need to target civilians in public, the desire for the entire world to see—it all pointed to a different purpose: propaganda.

Hitler didn't just want him dead—he wanted proof.

More than that, he would have wanted a way to display Captain America as a trophy.

As the whirring continued, the four short weapons barrels retreated from their outer mounts, reappearing on the inner corners where they could only aim at one thing: him. When he saw the reddish sparkle at their tips, Cap thought his long career might actually be over. But as they had been earlier, the beams that hit his pinned form were thin and weak, splashing along the anti-ballistic surface of his uniform almost like water. They were warm, heating his skin, but too slowly to cause blisters. Unseen fans began to churn, moving the air evenly around him and spreading the heat as if he were in a convection oven.

That was it. The cube was becoming an oven. The plan was clear now. It was going to bake him, dry his body without causing too much damage, then parade his mummified corpse across the world. The baking soda was intended to absorb additional moisture. But the suit membrane kept the powder from absorbing his sweat, leaving it to gather along his body. It began to boil.

An image of Kade flashed in his mind, disappointed that the temperature would not be hot enough to destroy the virus.

The warm sensation spreading over him tipped toward a dull, increasing pain. His body wanted to writhe, but he used the adrenaline for another try at the restraints. Every inch of his enhanced muscles grew taut. He pulled all four limbs at once with strength that had, in extreme circumstances, bent steel.

No good.

A different sort of grinding joined the whirs and clicks. Like topsy-turvy window shades, transparent walls rose from the bottom of the cube's frame. The higher the walls got, the more impossible they seemed. The space from which the walls emerged wasn't nearly large enough to contain their height. The glass-like substance must be some sort of liquid that solidified on exposure to air.

The purpose was no mystery: encasing him with the heat would aid the mummification process—and make for a better display.

Worsening pain made it harder to think. The constant agony had become every bit as intense as the brief scalding that had forced him to drop the hot shield.

The shield was still out in the sand, reminding him he had one trick left to play. His wrists were immobile, but his fingers could reach the activation pad in his palm. That would send the shield flying toward him. If it landed between his body and the beams, it might deflect them back against the cube.

But the magnetic return was designed with the assumption he'd be mobile enough to catch the returning disc. Its aerodynamics were so expertly fashioned, it could rip through any number of obstacles to reach the glove. With his limbs turned outward, one of those obstacles would be his arm.

Time was running out. If he waited until the cube was fully sealed, the shield might shatter one of the clear walls, but if they were at all flexible, the shield would bounce off. On the other hand, if he waited until the wall had *almost* sealed, the disc could keep it from closing.

Waiting for the right moment wasn't easy. The steady heat had made his skin a bristling mass of agony. He gnashed his teeth, surprised by how hot they felt against his tongue. Shaking, he tried to judge the speed of the shield against the rising of the wall, imagining the path and the angle.

It could work. It could.

As long as he didn't pass out...as long as he pressed the pad right about...

...now.

The shield flipped into the air, generating a small sand cloud. It ate the arid, empty distance between itself and the cube. As it neared, he worried it was traveling too low, that it would slam uselessly against the base of the cube.

But it didn't. It hit just right, wedging itself between the rising wall and the cube's frame.

It worked, but only partly.

While it prevented the wall from sealing, it hadn't reached the beams. If he'd delayed the inevitable at all, it was only by moments. The heat continued unabated. He'd played his last trick. Knowing S.H.I.E.L.D. was watching from the Helicarrier, he wondered whether Nia was among the observers. But even so, he felt alone.

Fury, where are you?

The answer came a second later. A thick blast, as black as the sand was white, slammed the exposed edge of the shield. Like a blade of grass tearing hrough a solid oak in a hurricane, the disc snapped upwards with such speed and force, it pried off the top of the cube.

What was left of the Sleeper exploded. Rogers couldn't be sure what caused it—a second shot from the Helicarrier, or some self-destruct mechanism sent him, along with the pieces of his former cage, flying high. The concussive wave that pressed his back was hotter and sharper than what he'd experienced inside the cube—but even through the strained membrane, the air ahead felt like a cold breeze.

The loose slats, still wrapped around his wrists and ankles, made landing more awkward than it had to be, but he wasn't any less relieved.

He rose to his knees and took a few long, cooling breaths. Ten yards away, the ground was scorched. The larger pieces in the debris field were still smoking. He stood, stretched, and checked his comm.

"Nick, you hear me?"

"Loud and clear."

"It was hot in there. What took you so long?"

"Once it retracted those beams, it didn't seem to have any offensive capacities, but we still couldn't take a shot without risking you. Your shield gave us something to hit. We aimed at the star, and the rest is history."

"Good to know."

"By the way, while you were playing shake and bake, my idea about replicating the Sleeper's bio sensors worked out. At first all we detected was you—the Sleepers' range seems pretty limited, which explains why they didn't go after the Skull, too—but when we increased their range by running it through the microwave antennae array, we got a blip. We found the Skull. Turns out Schmidt's got himself an actual castle in Roscoe, New York."

"So, good news?"

"I wish. Agent Velez in Signals has been on a roll, so I had her review any satellite data from that location during the last few months. Up until three days ago, at least thirty people occupied that space. Following some thermal activity inconsistent with the weather, every bio-form aside from the Skull was gone. Some atmospheric anomalies above the site yielded trace chemicals consistent with human ash."

"He incinerated his followers." Steve felt a twinge of pity for the dead before acknowledging the implications. "He must have done it to prevent the spread. So, the virus he has is an active strain?"

"That's one explanation, probably the best. Still, knowing the high regard the Skull has for human life, they could've burnt his breakfast strudel. Kade's having kittens, though, convinced the end of the world is nigh. Hell, he could be right. But we can chitchat about it once we reach our base. It's only four miles out. I'll send the drone to pick you up. Enjoy the free air while you can. There'll be a biohazard suit on board in case the membrane's ruptured."

Rogers looked out at the flat, lifeless expanse and blue sky. "If it's all the same to you, I think I'll walk."

ZO

Wanting to preserve that beauty can't be pointless.

THE BASALT cavern, previously used for storing old records, had been hastily repurposed. For obvious reasons, the Level 4 isolation area was the first of the new modular constructs placed there by the S.H.I.E.L.D. engineering crews. Other modules contained various workspaces for command and support, but this one—the largest and most expensive—held three quarantine chambers, each fairly roomy. Rogers' chamber even sported a window, though all it showed was a black stone wall.

But his mind didn't dwell on his surroundings. He was focused on the Red Skull and Jacobs' report. Returned to active duty since Paris, the wounded agent was part of the reconnaissance team in New York. As he spoke, his image—one of nine on the built-in floor-to-ceiling monitors—expanded to fill most of the screen. Aside from several stitched cuts and a slight paleness, he seemed to have recovered well.

"Without actual confirmation of an active pathogen, the CDC won't publicly declare it a hot zone, but we're treating it that way—expanding the perimeter around the Skull's castle up to two miles past the property boundaries, and evacuating homes and businesses. It's on about one thousand wooded acres. Access was easily sealed, but he's dug in tighter than the Latverian embassy. We know from satellite infrared that he's the only bio-form, but an EMF source is messing with our electronic surveillance equipment. Autonomous drones record a gray haze. We even tried getting an LMD closer via the sewers, with the same result. Honestly, I have no idea what other defenses he's got set up in there."

Jacobs' image shrank, while Fury's expanded. "Aside from Dr. Kade's suggestion that we drop a thermal bomb in the middle of New York state just to be on the safe side, are we all agreed we need boots on the ground to make an extraction?" He waited until the sundry faces nodded. "Okay. And speaking of everyone's favorite epidemiologist, Kade, you want to give us your surprising conclusion on who you, Dr. N'Tomo, *and* the CDC think should be wearing those boots?"

Kade's expanded image was striking, highlighting both his facial scars and an increasing weariness. He rubbed his eyes. "If logic seems surprising, Colonel, how do you judge the norm? Assuming the virus is active, it's only common sense to minimize the possibility of an outbreak. We can do that by sending someone who already carries it: Captain Rogers. If the Skull's virus is a different strain, it does put Rogers at added risk. On the other hand, whatever's keeping it inert in him could do the same for a variation. That's not something I can say about anyone else on the planet. And the fact that the membrane held indicates it would reduce his potential exposure."

Fury's face returned. "For someone in quarantine, he sure as hell gets around a lot. Which brings us to the Schrodinger's elephant in the room. If Schmidt *is* symptomatic, what do we do with him? Given that EMF, there won't be any communication, so it'll be Cap's call."

Kade spoke up again. "Captain Rogers, I want to remind you of our earlier conversation. It's a matter of history that you'd sooner die than risk innocent lives. When it comes down to it, will you value the Skull's life more than the lives of those a pandemic would rob?"

Steve blanched. "You may be confident about the outcomes, but to me only God knows the future. However educated our guesses are, all we've really got to go on is the moment—and in the moment, it would still be murder. I'm not going to go in and just kill him."

Kade rubbed his eyes again. "We're quibbling over semantics. Dr. N'Tomo, would you kindly summarize the document I forwarded to you?"

Nia's image widened. Looking uncomfortable, she cleared her throat. "About two hours ago, the International Court convened and sentenced Johann Schmidt, in absentia, to death. Captain Steve Rogers has been authorized to act as an official instrument of the court. As such, he is hereby given the explicit directive to carry out this sentence as quickly and as mercifully as possible."

SECONDS after Zola withdrew the syringe from Schmidt's arm, the details of the dim room grew more visible, the colors more vivid. He felt as strong as ever. Zola stepped back, but his sensors remained trained on the Skull.

"Watching for side effects?"

"This amount of adrenaline would induce a heart attack in a normal man. But your body is…"

"Not normal. *Ja*, I know."

Schmidt fully intended to lose the coming battle, but only in the same sense the Sleepers had "lost." Hindered by the bulky hazmat suits they'd no doubt be forced to wear, even S.H.I.E.L.D.'s best agents stood little chance against him. He would have to let them capture and isolate him. Still, if he gave up too easily, they might suspect his plan. Some sort of fight was necessary.

Perhaps he'd try to infect a few.

Hoping he'd be imprisoned near the dormant weapons was a gamble—but wherever S.H.I.E.L.D. brought him, he'd be in a better position to locate them. And then, who knows? If S.H.I.E.L.D. did have a cure, perhaps he'd allow them give it to him. *Then* he could use the Sleepers to destroy his hated foe anyway.

"How do you feel?"

The left side of his lips twitched into a half-smile. "As if I could live forever."

Zola's avatar mimicked the expression. "The effects of epinephrine normally last about twenty minutes, but this is my own formulation. Certain additives form a casing that will steadily release the drug over time. The full effect should last three hours. After that, I'm afraid your metabolism will crash precipitously. It is highly advisable that your encounter with S.H.I.E.L.D. be resolved by then."

Rolling down his sleeve, Schmidt nodded. A sudden darkness over his shoulder drew his attention to the monitors. The news feeds had gone dead.

"They've cut the fiber optics. I'm surprised it took as long as it did. The hardwired security system has yet to detect any incursions, but it won't be long now."

Donning his gloves, the Skull lifted the Sonikey. Having carefully wrapped it in a microfiber material that would conceal it from most sensors, he placed it in his mouth. Raising his glass to Zola, he washed it down with another Pilsner. "Time you were leaving."

"Understood, *Herr* Schmidt."

Rubbing his bony wrists beneath the leather, Schmidt surveyed the odd figure who had been his doctor and companion. "I feel I should thank you for standing by my side, but gratitude never sat easily with me."

He thought he detected a shrug in the digitized voice. "While such principles are more properly based on anticipated outcomes rather than sentimentality, I do admit to my own feelings about our parting. I have that luxury. You, however, must be at your best to face the coming days, and I have no wish to leave you at any disadvantage. Perhaps a different sort of confession on my part will make this parting easier."

Relieved there'd be no displays of emotion, the Skull embraced a far more comfortable curiosity. "A confession? From you? Any betrayal on your part would have already spelled my doom. What possible confession could you have?"

"Simply that I withheld information. I was often convinced you had become completely irrational, that your plan would never work. But I said nothing about this to you."

The Skull tilted his head. "Why not? You've disagreed with me before."

He heard that digital shrug again. This time it was tinged with a bit of...sheepishness?

"I thought it best to humor you."

"*Humor* me?"

"Yes…as a kindness toward a dying man."

The Skull seethed, his anger propelled by the artificial adrenaline, as Zola knew it would be.

"There, you see? I have removed the need for any gratitude on your part, and replaced it with the anger you believe fuels your will."

Heart pounding like a jackhammer, Schmidt fought to speak. "Indeed. You have. And for that, I freely thank you."

With the calm of a lazy wind-up toy, the android stepped toward the door. "I will head to the sub-basement, heat my body temperature to 300 degrees Celsius to destroy any trace of the virus, then exit through the tunnel. I doubt they've been able to detect me, but I've minimized my energy signature so that I should remain invisible to their scanners even after I've left the protection of the EMF." His body remained facing the hall, but the lens that acted as his eyes pivoted back. "Goodbye, Johann."

Schmidt clicked his heels and gave him a stiff bow. "Arnim."

The reinforced door closed. The latch engaged with a click. The Skull's gaze lingered on it until the sound of heavy footsteps in the hall receded, then he turned to watch Zola's progress on the monitors.

While Arnim walked, his body glowed as red as the coils on an electric stove. When he reached the sealed sub-basement, he stood motionless until his cooling body returned to its usual hues, then vanished through the escape tunnel.

To conserve battery power, the Skull switched off everything but the few functioning monitors and sat.

Alone.

Alone with his failing body. Alone with the sterile air. Alone with his will in the unending darkness.

And with the artificial adrenaline pumping through his veins, he thought, *This must be what God felt like in the moments before creation.*

21

Not to appreciate beauty, well, that would be the very definition of pointlessness.

YELLOW, pink, and orange: The wafting cloud bed beneath Steve Rogers was tinged with sunset colors. Jumping from the hover-flier, he arched downward in a perfect dive. He might've felt an exhilarating sense of freedom, but his assignment prevented any appreciation of the view.

He'd been asked to kill someone.

Not that he disagreed with the court's verdict. There was no higher political authority, the stakes were as high as they could get—and Schmidt was a vile, heinous thing. If the Skull was sick, dying anyway, and the virus threatened humanity, he had to at least consider it, didn't he?

But would he even have killed Hitler, given the opportunity?

To him, that was hardly an abstract question, nothing like Kade's hypothetical train wreck. The Allies, and his own generals, had made attempts—but asking him to be the assassin would never have occurred to them. First and foremost, they knew he'd refuse. Beyond that, even the most cynical military leader was well aware of Captain America's value as a symbol.

He held the title of captain, but was never exactly rank-and-file. He took on missions that made sense to him, but only served America's dream. That meant more than obeying any particular administration or any particular orders.

As he plunged into the cloud cover, its pristine beauty disappeared. As with any dream, the devil was in the details. Up close, the sublime colors faded into a dank, gray fog. It sped past, wetting his uniform and the membrane.

Kade's last question echoed: "Will you value the Skull's life more than the lives of those a pandemic would rob?"

If the Skull were aiming a gun at a civilian or about to detonate a bomb, and the only way to stop him was to end him, Rogers wouldn't hesitate. But that would be combat, not an execution.

Was that enough of a difference?

They'd meet soon enough, and Steve Rogers would find out what he would do. In the heat of combat, it might not even be an issue. He'd been in many battles after which his foe did not walk away.

The cloud cover dissipated, and the castle came into view: a piece of Old Europe dropped on the New World. Instinct told him it was time to pull the ripcord, but he held back. It would make for a rougher landing, but he wanted to remain hard to see for as long as possible.

The whole world had seen him wearing the hazmat suit and using the Iron Man armor bearing a hologram of his face. Others could guess at the reason, but the Skull would know it was because of the virus they shared. While he'd be expecting *someone*, Schmidt might not expect his oldest foe in the flesh.

Before his increasing acceleration could ensure more than minor bruising, he snapped the cord. The ram-air chute fanned out, its cloaking material reflecting the darkening skies. The hover-flier had been well placed for the jump. Despite the speed of his descent, he barely had to steer to reach the sloped roof.

In a maneuver that would have cracked bones in a normal body, Cap waited until he was five yards up, then released his harness, letting it and the chute flap into the wind. He hit the slate shingles a little harder than expected and rolled along the slant to the base of a high stone chimney. As he crouched in its shadow, broken bits of slate skittered by, falling three stories before thudding into the bushes below.

A mounted gun rose from the chimney top, erupting with automatic-weapons fire. It wasn't targeting him, though—it was aimed at the still-fluttering chute, which it shredded. And the old castle didn't have just one chimney, it had six—each now topped with a similar weapon. The red dots of their laser sighting crossed over the roof and grounds. The lack of additional fire meant he hadn't been spotted yet.

The Skull was somewhere inside, either operating the guns remotely or trusting whatever auto-targeting system they possessed. But where was he? The castle had two wings. Rogers had landed in the rough center of the shorter. On either side, several dormers projected from the sloping roof. Fading sunlight gave him a glimpse inside the closest window, illuminating what looked like an empty, rotting hall.

Knowing that where the Skull was concerned, things were seldom as they seemed, Cap took his shield from his back and sent it crashing through the window. The instant it cracked the glass, the illusion of an empty hall vanished. A series of flamethrowers erupted, starting at the corridor's far end and meeting the flying disc midway.

Auto-targeting, then.

The shield sailed the remaining length, crashed back out a second dorme, and returned to his waiting hand. It was cool to the touch. Inside, only lingering flames licked the edges of the lightly charred molding. The system was set to fire only as long as an intruder was present.

Was the Skull too ill to see to his own defense, or planning some other surprise?

The flamethrowers also told him something else. Logically, the firing sequence would end closest to whatever the weapons were intended to protect. In this case, that was a door leading to the other wing. He looked across the roof: Beyond more dormers, the outer wall rose to a wide peak with tall windows. The large room beyond appeared to be abandoned, but that was probably just another projection.

And it seemed as good a place as any to start his search. If he stayed low and moved fast, he might make it in without tripping any sensors.

No such luck.

The second he left the chimney's shadow, all the mounted guns swiveled and fired at him. Heavy-gauge bullets hit his raised shield and the surrounding slate, shattering the roof covering to reveal a layer of armor beneath.

He ran for it, the gunfire strafing his path. By the time he reached the end of the western roof, the hail of bullets made the windows in the east wing barely visible. Scores of hot projectiles plinking off his shield, he made a catty-corner leap. Cap expected it to take him through the glass, but steel grates rolled across the windows as he jumped.

He hit one of the grates, grabbed hold, and swung to the side. He might be able to pry it off, but not while weathering this heavy fire. The barrage was already tearing out chunks of castle stone, hitting far too close to his hands. He'd have to neutralize the guns before he tried getting in—but that would give the Skull more time to prepare.

Unless…he did both at once?

Vaulting to the base of the nearest chimney, he landed so close its gun couldn't target him. That didn't stop the others. Round after round followed him as he climbed to the chimney top and wedged his shield into the gun mount.

No longer able to turn, the machinery whined, but the gun continued firing. Turning his shield, he was able to aim it. His first target was the gun with the most direct line of sight on the covered windows. That chimney tilted and fell.

The remaining weapons were still shooting, but he didn't want to give Schmidt any extra breathing space. His next target wasn't the protective steel grates on the windows, but what surrounded them. Once enough stone was blasted away, he sprang toward the grate a second time.

He hit feet first, delivering enough force to collapse what remained of the support frame. The grate fell inward. With a great thud, he and it landed on the marble floor of a wide, dark room. The sound of gunfire ringing behind him, he stood in a cloud of powdered stone and plaster, ready to hurl his shield at the familiar figure standing stiffly behind a cracked oaken desk.

The Skull was speaking, but his words were drowned out by the commotion. Grimacing, he swiped at a control. The guns fell silent.

"That's better," the Skull said. Narrowing his eyes, he tilted his domed head. "So it's you, not some surrogate. But you don't seem sick at all. Why is that?"

"I like to think it's clean living."

He frowned. "I understand the need for wit that some of your fellow costumed cretins possess—but your naive idealism always makes me wonder if you're capable of being facetious. If clean living can keep one healthy, how do you explain all the placid, innocent sheep who die daily from disease? Is their living not clean enough for you?"

Schmidt still hadn't moved. The light from the monitor glowing behind him made it difficult to see his face clearly. Was he weak, or biding his time?

"They don't have the same kind of body we do."

"*Ach*, of course." Bowing slightly, the Skull took on the paper-thin mask of an ingratiating host welcoming an old friend. "Touché."

Schmidt's German accent was back. Rogers hadn't heard it in a very long time. An effect of the virus?

"Well, I've been having a lot of philosophical debates lately."

The thin, dreadful lips made something akin to a *tsk-tsk*. "How hard that must be for a simple mind like yours."

When he stepped out from behind the desk, Rogers tensed. The Skull moved slowly, keeping his gloved hands visible. His posture was rigid. There were no nervous twitches, no wavering, no wasted motion that might telegraph his intentions—or tremors that could indicate disease. To judge from his self-control, he seemed in perfect health.

But his face, when Rogers finally saw it, told a different story. Not its thin scarlet skin or skull-like shape, not its corpse-cold expression or malevolent glare, but the patches of discoloration on his temples and cheeks, and the lines of liquid red between his teeth.

There was no question anymore. The virus was active.

"There was a time I thought dying might be worth it just to rid myself of the unfortunate association between us. But seeing you so healthy, so fit, I find myself forced to ask—has a cure been found?"

Rogers shook his head. "No. Not yet. I have the virus, but it's not active in me."

Hearing that, the Skull laughed long and hard. "You mean you've been fighting the Sleepers in this ridiculous fashion because of what *might* happen?"

"What we've got, it could—"

"*Ja, ja,* I know. Threaten the species. Yet, after remaining dormant all these years, it has only activated in me. It almost makes me wonder if there is some design to the universe."

Schmidt seemed oddly introspective. Maybe if he was captured easily, Rogers could convince Kade and the courts that keeping him alive would be useful in finding a cure. "You must know everyone we've got is working on this. Turn yourself in, submit to quarantine, let them test you. I don't expect you to care about saving anyone else, but it's the only way to save yourself."

The Skull waved a gloved hand in the air, curled his lips in a sort of pout, and took a few steps closer. At first, his words were slow and deliberate. "*Nein.* That won't be happening. I admit, I did consider it. But now, with you here? No. I won't do it. Not for you. Never for you."

All of a sudden he was screeching: "Cure or not, I will never humble myself before *you!*"

The Skull threw himself forward. Rogers was taken aback by his speed and ferocity. Their bodies the same, he expected that at most the Skull would be *as* fast as he was, *as* strong.

Somehow, he was faster. Stronger.

He raised his shield to block, but the Skull knocked it aside. He jabbed with his right, but the Skull slammed the top of his head into Rogers' nose before the blow could connect. The unexpected energy behind the strike staggered him. Salty liquid seeped into the back of his throat. He caught a whiff of his own blood.

As he shook it off, Rogers promised himself he wouldn't be caught off-guard again.

Cackling madly, the Skull came at him, feinting a body blow before he hit the ground for a low-spinning heel kick. Fast as it was, it didn't come close. Rogers jumped. The Skull's leg swept the air, the flaps of his open black leather trench coat splaying to his sides.

Thinking to pin him by the fabric and interrupt his momentum, Rogers came down on the coat. As if he'd hit an oil slick, the balls of his feet flew out from under him.

The Skull chuckled. "You'd think such a long garment would be a poor choice for hand-to-hand combat. But mine was inspired by the carnivorous pitcher plant, whose slippery leaves cause its prey to helplessly slide into its digestive juices."

The advantage was momentary. Rogers easily regained his balance. The tiny delay shouldn't have given the Skull the time to stand—but it did. How?

Whatever body he inhabited, despite the martial arts he'd mastered, the Skull was at heart a street fighter, a thuggish scrapper with a heavy reliance on dirty tricks. But something else was going on here, something even beyond the capabilities of the Super-Soldier serum. The best way to end the fight would be to figure out what that was.

Hoping to get a closer look at his foe's tactics, Cap let Schmidt keep the advantage. The Skull came at him with an amateur move: a roundhouse punch. Rogers sidestepped, grabbed his wrist, and used the motion to push the slick sleeve of the coat along the Skull's forearm. It slid easily, but the sudden force made it tear as it went.

The Skull twisted and yanked free. But in the scant moments Rogers' hand had been wrapped around Schmidt's bare forearm, he'd felt the veins beneath the skin pounding as if ready to burst.

A drug. He was using some sort of drug.

As far back as Dr. Erskine, Steve Rogers had been warned that the effects of a stimulant, unlike alcohol, would increase exponentially in his enhanced body. That included a dangerous side effect: a heightened irritability that would interfere with his concentration. That explained the roundhouse.

Schmidt was already too angry to think straight. All Rogers had to do was make him furious, and more mistakes would follow.

The Skull wheeled toward him, trying to use his left to swipe the shield aside again. That exposed his head and upper chest. Suppressing the urge to counter with his right, Rogers forced the edge of the shield up into the Skull's chin—knowing it would cause more pain.

Howling, the Skull tumbled back.

"Never humble yourself? Who do you think you're kidding?" Rogers said. "This is for show. You're barely fighting. You're like any other bully, a coward at heart. You've spent your whole life terrified. Fear is the only thing that's ever driven you."

Wild-eyed, Schmidt came at him. "Save the dime-store psychology for the mewling masses."

Rogers let him in without resistance, allowed blow after blow to land on his chest and sides.

"Does *this* feel like *fear*?" Schmidt bayed.

It didn't. In fact, it hurt. A lot. But powerful as the strikes felt, they were scattershot, purposeless.

The yellowed eyes went even wider. "Does a tiger *fear* his prey?"

The flurry of punches peaked and continued, but Rogers heard Schmidt panting above the thudding fists. "Is it *fear* when the predator trembles at the taste of his living prey quivering between his teeth?"

Rogers had taken about as much as he could. The Skull was leaving himself wide open. Cap was about to counter, hopefully take out the villain in one shot. But the uncanny strength behind the cascading blows subsided, and Cap paused, biding his time.

Caught in some sort of fit, Schmidt struggled to breathe, sucking in and expelling air in increasingly shallow bursts. "I am the hunter! The world is my prey!"

His fists flailed more than struck. His bulging eyes looked ready to burst. By the time the last feeble punches hit, Rogers was able to comfortably straighten his back.

"It will…not ever…be *me* who lies…begging…in those jaws…it will be…"

Schmidt raised his fist once more, but then the whole of his body rattled. He bent over, shivering. His throat emitted a horrible wheeze. One quivering hand was splayed on the star of Rogers' chest; with the other Schmidt grasped his own chest.

Schmidt went to his knees. "…it…will be…"

Rogers took a step back, letting the Skull collapse to the floor. Schmidt's arms swam in what was left of his coat sleeves. The wheezing fell to silence.

Now. Now was the time. From the look of him, Schmidt wouldn't have much longer anyway. Considering the pain on the red twitching face, it might even be a mercy. He could end this, quickly and cleanly.

But try as he might to embrace the reasoning, Steve knew in his heart it had never been a question.

He turned to the cracked desk and shut down the castle defenses, including the EMF. The area was already being treated as a Level 4 hot zone, but he'd have to warn S.H.I.E.L.D. he was taking a prisoner. Then it would be up to Kade and Nia to figure out how to transport him.

Rogers withdrew two restraining bands from his belt. As he bent over the still figure, an odd thought occurred to him.

Maybe they'd put them both in cryogenic suspension. Side by side.

Sickened by the thought, he was about to bind Schmidt's ankles when the Skull kicked into the marble floor. Arms free of the coat's slick sleeves, he slid along the fabric, taking cover behind the desk. Having caught what remained of his breath, he rose, lifted half the desk, and hurled it.

Rogers ducked, but the splintered edge caught his side, sending him into a half-spin. That gave the Skull just enough time to fire two shots. Whether he'd had the gun on him all along, or had retrieved it from the desk, it didn't matter now. The first shot ricocheted off Cap's shield. The second tore through his uniform at the shoulder.

Armor-piercing bullets.

The Skull spat more than spoke. "You had me. Why didn't you kill me?"

"I'm not a murderer."

"*Feiger hund!* You've killed often enough. In the war, your suppressing fire hit many foot soldiers who cared more about getting home than they did about serving my cause."

"They chose their side when they picked up the gun. But I don't expect you to understand. Your kind never cares who you hit, or when—soldier or civilian."

The Skull shrugged. "Inefficient, I grant you, but it does make aiming easier." He fired again, missing completely. "But you stood over me for so long, you must have at least been thinking about compromising your beloved ideals."

"Not for a moment."

The Skull tilted his head, studying his face. "Who is lying now? But those you serve are far more pragmatic. Did they order you to capture me alive?"

Rogers' expression hadn't changed at all, but the Skull saw something in it all the same. "They didn't, did they? They wanted me dead. And you *disobeyed*? Ha!"

His smile grew nearly wide enough to bring a semblance of life to the death's head.

"*Der Führer* was wrong about your importance, then and now. You've always been more *dorftrottel* than national hero." The Skull dropped the gun and held up his hands. "Under the circumstances, I surrender—if only because it will vex you further."

*But believing in beauty doesn't mean risking my life
for it, does it?*

THE HOVER-FLIER slowed as if to land, but it looked to N'Tomo as if they were still in the middle of nowhere. All she could see from the window was a fallen road sign indicating there'd been a road here once, one with a sharp curve ahead. The sign seemed new, the dry desert air an impediment to rust, but it was probably many decades old—like Steve Rogers. Otherwise, the view was all flatlands and big sky, like Somalia's thorn-bush savannah. The place where they'd met was very similiar to the place where they'd likely part.

Full circle, then.

She expected the hover-flier to set down on the ground. Instead, a rectangular section of the sand slid away, revealing a dark cavern below.

"Holographic projection," Fury explained. "Kinda like what the Skull had at his place. Same reason, too. Course, tech's all well and good, but I always found this next part more impressive."

As the hover-flier descended, the cavern walls came into view, revealing their exquisite shape as a series of tall, six-sided stone pillars. They were as geometrically perfect in their way as the Sleepers.

"That hexagonal structure is natural. The whole place is basalt, formed by lava flows about 15 million years ago. The excavation was careful to preserve it because it acts as a support structure. And it's pretty, too."

She gave him a look. Never having heard Fury speak about anything other than strategies and tactics, Nia was pleasantly surprised.

Fury noticed. "Yeah, I know something about geology. What of it, doc?"

"It's beautiful, but I can see why we used the hover-flier. The cargo area here is smaller than the one on the Helicarrier."

"Cargo area? You're looking at the whole base. It was just a buncha redundant files that've already been digitized, pretty much abandoned since the eighties." He grimaced at Kade. "Even spies like us don't bother coming here anymore."

"So much the better for our purposes," Kade said.

The black walls were lit by sporadic floodlights, but the space below glowed with white box rooms and tubular corridors.

"It's no broom closet. Plenty of space for the containment area, a state-of-the-art lab, support offices, and so on. Even had enough room to establish a sterile zone for the Sleeper wreckage," Fury said, adding in a low grumble, "at your insistence."

The hover-flier maneuvered toward one of the few open areas and set down.

Kade grumbled back. "*I* asked that you incinerate them, in case they carry any virus spores as a result of their encounters with Captain Rogers."

The rear hatch opened. "We will, soon as we're done studying them. If we hadn't created detailed files on the original Sleepers, we might never have defeated these—so it's important. But trust me, they'll be long gone before we activate the...uh, cryo-chamber."

Nia felt a little shudder. "Both patients are in place?"

Fury led them out. "Patients. Yeah. They share a wall, but they can't see each other—so no reason to tell them that. Steve's watching footage of his fight with the cube, in case we missed anything. The Skull was transported here in a modified biohazard shipping container, based on your specs. He stayed in it until we let him out into his cozy new home. He's been cooperative, if you call doing absolutely nothing 'cooperative.' Come to think of it, in his case, I guess you can."

Walking in the open cavern, he pointed to a particularly thick metal door in the containment pod. Two agents wearing hazmat suits stood outside, weapons at the ready. "Dressing room's over there. I'll be watching from the command center."

Nia took several steps toward the door before noticing Kade was scrutinizing the module. "Shall we suit up?"

She tapped him on the shoulder. Twice. "Doctor?"

"Yes. Of course."

Once inside the mod's first chamber, they began the tedious process of donning dual-layered hazmat suits. These were so thick and bulky they were nicknamed *spacesuits*. Though both doctors wore the experimental membranes, Kade insisted on following standard protocol as an added precaution. Nia didn't disagree, but had to ask, "Back there, were you searching for leaks?"

"It may seem foolish, but yes."

"Do you think you might actually be able to see any?"

"We always assume someone else will notice the obvious—a missing connector, a crack in a pipe—but I sometimes think more damage is done by incompetence than evil. Thanks to Rogers' misplaced ideals, we're dealing with a strain that's proven itself active. We're at a stage where it's impossible to be too careful. To that end, let's review the procedure before going in."

She nodded. "Once the patient is secured, we'll withdraw three vials of blood. The syringe will be immediately destroyed in the secure disintegrator. Two of the samples will be stored in the containment area. The third will be taken out, scanned for use in our computer modeling, and then destroyed."

They put on their helmets. The portable air supply activated, and the spacesuit fabric puffed up. If there were any holes or tears, the outward pressure would prevent pathogens from reaching the wearer. The loud, constant rush of the fans made Nia feel like a deep-sea diver, arms-distant from the world—and, hopefully, from anything that might contaminate her.

Their air supplies in one hand, their equipment in the other, they entered a windowless corridor. The door behind them closed. After a moment, the one ahead opened.

It led to the anteroom to Johann Schmidt's containment chamber, its transparent walls the final protection against the disease. When the Skull saw them, he came to attention. Having read so much about him, Nia wasn't sure what to expect. His head was disfigured, but not horrifically. Its resemblance to a naked skull might frighten others, but to someone who'd seen the human form ravaged by all manner of disease, he just looked very ill, unhealthily thin with indications of dehydration.

Kade activated the speakers. "Please sit in the chair."

With a curt little nod, Schmidt obeyed. Once he settled in, Kade pressed a second button. Thick straps—metal covered in soft plastic to prevent accidental cuts—snapped around his wrists, ankle, and neck. It reminded Nia of how experimental chimps were bound in less compassionate days. It felt cruel, and cruelty was something she reviled—even toward those who might deserve it.

With a hiss, the final door slid open, and they stepped inside.

The Skull looked at them both, but addressed the man who'd spoken to him. His voice carried into their helmets through a microphone embedded somewhere in the walls.

"Are the restraints necessary?"

Workmanlike, Kade rolled up the sleeve of the patient's gown. "Yes."

His arm was as muscular as Steve's, which was to be expected—but the skin was papery thin, almost translucent, like that of many victims of disease. Kade gave it no more than a passing glance before wrapping a rubber hose tightly around the brachium.

Without being asked, the Skull made a fist.

Almost as a reward, Kade explained himself. "During an epidemic of bubonic plague in Surat, we had a patient who purposely tried to smear his blood on the emergency workers. Three of my colleagues died."

"I have no reason to lash out at you."

"Neither did he." Swabbing the crook of the Skull's arm, Kade slapped the skin with two fingers, testing for veins. "And unlike you, he'd never harmed a soul in his life. In addition to liquefying his insides, one of the effects of the virus was to do the same to his personality. He became feral. Ever since, I've insisted on restraints."

With the quiet fascination of a child, the Skull watched the needle slip under his skin. "Understandable. I assume you would have preferred taking these samples from my corpse?"

"There are some benefits in observing the disease in a living host. Captain Rogers' decision to spare you was beyond foolish. That doesn't mean I should ignore any advantages it offers."

"On that much we agree, *Herr* doktor."

Nia handed Kade a second tube, then a third. When he withdrew the needle, he dabbed the wound with a cotton ball. Save for a single red drop, it was clean.

"His clotting is still normal," she said. "That's a good sign."

"Perhaps."

The walls contained two fixtures. The one facing the anteroom was a secure transfer unit. Locked from this side, it could be used to convey small items to the patient without breaching the containment. The other, on the cell's only blank white wall, seemed to lead nowhere.

It was also locked, until N'Tomo pressed a remote and a small drawer appeared. She placed the syringe and cotton ball inside. Another press closed the drawer. An electronic pop followed, telling her the contents hadn't simply been sterilized—they'd been disintegrated.

Schmidt watched, delighted. "Impressive! May I inquire as to your progress with the virus?"

He again spoke to Kade. Nia wondered whether the doctor would answer the way she would, trying instill a sense of hope, no matter how small. If it didn't set the patient's mind at ease, at least it might make future cooperation more likely. But Kade gave out the hard facts, unadorned.

"In your case, it would be irrelevant. The International Court has condemned you to death. Since Rogers refused to fulfill their decree, there's an executioner on the way who will perform his duties as soon as the base is secure."

Nia's eyes flared at Kade's stupidity.

The Skull blinked. "Even though I am already dying?"

"Your history renders you too much of a flight risk."

"I have no intention of going anywhere."

"That may well be the case, but the man who spit on his doctors had no such intentions, either."

The Skull shrugged and fell silent.

Their work complete, they exited. Fuming, N'Tomo waited until they were back in the corridor. As soon as the antechamber door sealed and UV lights bathed their suits, she turned on her colleague.

"Are you insane? Why on earth would you tell one of the world's most dangerous criminal minds that he has no reason not to try to escape?"

Kade grimaced. "Really, doctor, you wonder why I check for leaks when it's you who should be paying more attention. His pulse is low, he's feverish, and there was no strength in his arm at all. If he weren't faking health due to some misguided sense of propriety, he would have fallen before he reached the chair. The only things holding him up were the restraints. He isn't going anywhere."

KNOWING he was under constant surveillance, Schmidt remained seated after they left. It was difficult. When the effects of the epinephrine wore off during the maddening journey to this forsaken desert, he'd crashed hard, as Zola had warned. He had no doubt his captors realized his weakness. Allowing them to believe pride made him hide his vulnerability would make it more surprising when some of his strength did return. If they believed they'd discovered his lie, they'd be easier to fool.

The deceit gave him only a slight advantage—and though he was loathe to admit it, perhaps a pointless one. All his brilliant scheming may have done nothing more than deliver him into the hands of his enemies.

But why? Why weren't the Sleepers responding?

He knew they were here. When the guards marched him past the three sealed containers, he suspected what they held. A glance at a passing manifest confirmed it, filling him with confidence that his plan would actually succeed. But the mere presence of the Sonikey in his gut should have activated the final sequence, and though the Sleepers were still no more than 50 yards away, nothing had happened. Had the shielding that kept it from being detected also blocked its signal? Impossible. They'd compensated for that. What, then? He'd no idea what sort of marvel could possibly restore the broken heaps, but he'd seen what these Sleepers could do, and he'd believed in them, perhaps more than was wise.

Had the old technology simply failed? Now, of all times?

His rage still spent, another sensation crawled in through the cracks of his tired mind: resignation.

Even the most perfect dreams rust over time.

Perhaps Zola had been right all along: It really was over.

Then let it come at the hands of their executioner, rather than a *verdammt* virus. At least there'd be a purpose behind it: punishment for what the sheepish masses considered his crimes. He would still give them a last-minute surprise, take out as many of the dogs as possible—show them right up until the end what it means to live and die by acts of will.

The thought rallied him. He was feeling better, no longer worried he would slip from the chair to the floor. He might even be able to stand.

As his limbs slowly came back to life, his leg and arm muscles ached—the cost of his battle with Rogers. He needed to stretch, so he rose, careful to use both hands to push himself up, careful to waver so they'd think him unsteady. He looked at the white table, the white door, the white wall, and then out the glass wall at more white walls. The spot where the sterilization unit appeared was seamless, so tightly fitted it was invisible to the eye, but he remembered where it was. He might be able to access the disintegrator, turn it against his confines, but they would see him the moment he moved.

There was nothing to do but wait.

And wait.

They might have thought to provide some reading material.

And they thought *him* barbaric.

He was only standing for a few minutes when his abdomen tensed as if gripped in a vise, forcing him to bend over. At first he took the electric shiver for one of the spasms that had been plaguing him.

It wasn't, though. It was the Sonikey, vibrating inside him. But this was not the pulsing signal he expected. Muted as it was by the sheath, he still recognized the sound—the same it had made three times before. It could only mean one thing.

There was *another* Sleeper, a fourth.

And it was being awoken.

It wasn't over, then. Far from it.

He bent over even farther, but not because of the discomfort. He bent so they wouldn't see him smile.

23

But if I sacrifice myself, I do it in secret. Who would know?
Who would care?

WHAT was the word?

Freighted. That was it. That was how Jakob Waller felt about his life. Freighted. Even his own thoughts had grown too freighted, too familiar to interest him much.

He was alone in Vienna's Weltliche Schatzkammer Museum, in an elegant office. At work long after closing, he placed rare artifacts from the Holy Roman Empire beneath the magnifier one by one, scanning for signs of damage or decay—wishing he could do the same for himself.

They'd offered him the day off, but he refused. He'd hoped that spending time with things much older than he was might shake the gloom that had descended on him on the occasion of his 73rd birthday. As of yet, it had not.

The day wasn't a disappointment. It was more a verification of something he'd felt for a while: not that he'd outlived his usefulness, but that he'd outlived his desire to be useful.

Waller wasn't sad or lonely. His health was good and his mind sharp, or at least as sharp as it had ever been. He didn't lack social skills or compassion. It was just that now that he was old enough to really see how it would all inevitably end, he had no desire to make an effort anymore.

Friends and co-workers brought him a lovely Sachertorte, his favorite. They covered it with candles and sang to him with genuine affection. They were good people, kind and intelligent, but none knew him nearly as long or as well as those who were now long gone.

Going through the collection proved equally hollow. Once, each piece had enthralled him, rousing passion and dedication. Tonight, his long experience worked against him, blinding him to each artifact's glory, revealing the inconvenient truths his heart could no longer deny.

Instead of a unicorn relic, he saw a misidentified narwhal horn. Instead of the Holy Grail, he saw an agate bowl dated to Late Antiquity.

He knew too much about them. Or perhaps he knew too little.

Much as he longed for the magic of lies, their danger had grown too apparent, especially in the case of the piece he'd saved for last: the Holy Spear, Longinus. Europe's most real demon had seen the magic in it, all right. The vile Adolf Hitler once brought it back with him to Berlin, believing the so-called Spear of Destiny would secure his Eternal Reich.

Once, Waller thought it was harmless to believe in the spear's mystic properties, but Voltaire said it best: "Those who can make you believe absurdities can make you commit atrocities."

He turned over the lance in his hands. Its crude, pointed, flat metal head was strapped to the central pole that had a sheet of inscribed silver and gold wrapped around the center. Even General

Patton had it studied before returning it to the museum. Some blamed his death in a car accident a few months later on the Spear's power.

Today, all Jakob saw was a piece fashioned in the 7th century for ceremonial use. Another lie disguised as meaning. Another absurdity that aided and abetted atrocity.

About to place it beneath the magnifier, he was still holding it when the tremors began. At first he thought his steady hands were finally failing him, shaking like those of a stereotypical old man. But it wasn't his hands—it was the spear, shivering so violently he had to let go.

It clattered to the desk. Its vibrations sent it skittering across the surface, rattling his carefully stacked papers and organized colored pens.

Jakob wondered if what he was seeing was real, or if he was having a stroke and his body was telling him a final lie before death. But it felt as real as anything he'd experienced.

In a burst of golden light, the flattened blade and staff were shed as if parts of a vulgar costume, garish lipstick on the Mona Lisa.

What remained was perfect: a long, solid rod, narrow as an abstract line.

As Jakob gasped, it rose into the air, knocking the magnifier aside. Weightless, it spun like a compass needle seeking magnetic north. When it settled, it was pointing at him, directly at his chest, as if he'd been chosen by it. He felt that old thrill again—the idea that not only was there magic in the world, but that he might be part of it.

As the perfect thing drove itself into and through Jakob Waller, all the experiences, expectations, and explanations that had rendered his life so dull and gray shattered as quickly and easily as his chest. He saw his elegant office before him, heard the wall behind him crack as the rod passed through it. Then nothing.

Smiling, Jakob Waller died just as he'd been born: believing that he and the world were completely new.

THE BIG EMPTY'S modular command center was as white and sterile as the rest of the base. To Kade, it felt soothing, clean, but it also made any variation look like dirt. As a result, he found himself staring at Fury's unshaven chin. The stubble wrankled him nearly as much as the cowboy's habitual bravado.

"I feel like I'm in a freaking habitrail," Fury said, rapping his knuckles against the featureless wall. "Guess I shouldn't complain. At least we got a table in here, so I can see most of your kissers up close and personal." He looked at the gathered group, then two faces appearing on the built-in wall monitors. "Weird seeing you up there when you're just 50 yards away, Cap, but at least you've got your own monitor. Congrats."

Playing along, Rogers gave him a salute. "Thank you, sir."

"What about me?" Stark piped in. "Don't I have my own monitor?"

"Yeah, I just don't feel like congratulating one of the world's richest men on that. I do wanna thank you for showing your virtual mug all the way from sunny Silicon Valley."

Kade didn't get it. Did they have to whistle in the dark, to pretend? Didn't they realize how difficult it made it for him, for anyone with half a brain, to trust them?

"Let's get down to it. In about two hours, when the court's, uh, *instrument* arrives, Schmidt will legally be placed under his jurisdiction and summarily executed." Looking at Kade, he added, "Frankly, I'd as soon say they're going to whack him."

Kade wondered if the remark was intended to make him feel guilty. If so, how? They were the ones caught up in appearances. It didn't make any difference to him what they called it, as long as Schmidt was dead and the pestilence inside him eradicated.

Fury finally muted his glib tone when he arrived at the meeting's purpose. "Once the Skull's cremated, Steve Rogers will be placed in the cryo-chamber. That makes this meeting our last official chance for any of our best and brightest to pull a rabbit out of a hat or wake me up and tell me I've been dreaming before we actually go through with this. Have we got anything? Anything at all? Doctors, let's start with you."

Kade said nothing. He'd let Dr. N'Tomo report for them. She was competent enough, and they appreciated her manner. More important, she could only discuss what she knew, and Kade had yet to decide whether he should share his most recent discovery.

She cleared her throat. "First, I'd like to ask if Mr. Stark's presence indicates he's made any progress."

"It's Tony, totally Tony. I guess the question means *your* report isn't good, so I'm sorry to say no. If creating cures by computer sim were all that easy, we'd have eliminated lots of diseases by now. So far I'm limited to crunching algorithms to speed the calculations. Every microsecond I squeeze out could be the one that gives us a winner, but nothing's screaming Bingo yet. I'm only here as a sounding board, or maybe a charming cheer squad. So...yay. Go team."

Fury gestured toward Nia. "What *have* you got?"

Her face grew dour. "The samples from the Skull have revealed that his symptoms are being caused by a very *slight* variation on the virus. The variation itself is no surprise. Viruses constantly mutate—usually into less harmful forms. So far, though, the simulations show that this variation is even *more* contagious and *more* resistant to cure." She took a moment before continuing. "We also now know it's keyed to specific cellular modifications caused by the Super-Soldier formula."

Fury raised an eyebrow. "Does that mean it *can't* infect the rest of us?"

"No," she said. "Not at all. We know from its structure that we're all susceptible. The same key can work on more than one lock. In this case, the key that opens up a Super-Soldier cell can also unlock an average human cell."

Kade wasn't surprised when Fury pushed for more. "I was shot down when I asked this the first time, but we're here to brainstorm, so I'll try again—could this thing have been *created* to target Cap? We've seen stranger."

More tired than he realized, Kade could not hold his tongue. "Finding a villain may make for a more comfortable story, Colonel, but it isn't in any way necessary to explain what's happened."

They all turned toward him, expecting him to continue, but he forced himself to say nothing further. Drained, rattled by what he now knew, he feared he might say too much, or be misinterpreted. Besides, what tired him most had been trying to explain.

N'Tomo continued for him. "It may seem like an intelligence is behind it, but this is more about luck. When a million random lock picks try to open the same lock, it's only the one that succeeds that gets to reproduce. Naturally, just as an active virus in my body is more likely to be specific to my immune system, an active virus in the Skull's clonedbody is more likely to be specific to Super-Soldier DNA."

Fury bristled. "I'm still not buying the part about—"

A frantic Stark interrupted. His eyes had zeroed in on an unseen point beyond his camera. "Whoa! You got that, Nick?"

Before Fury could answer, yet another monitor—this one built into the tabletop—lit with tracking information.

"Getting it from the Helicarrier now. There's a bogie headed our way—fast. Point of origin is Vienna."

Rogers tensed. "Another Sleeper?"

Stark shrugged. "I'd say that's a bet. This one's big, too. Well, not very big at all, really. It's pretty small, maybe five feet long, and crazy thin—but when I say big, I mean powerful."

Kade felt sick. Another attack. Of course. Another inexorable force pressing them all closer to the brink. He hid his shaking hands beneath the table.

Fury hit the alert button, which was actually red and labeled *alert*. "The energy readings we're getting are off the scale."

Stark smirked. "Speak for yourself. With all the big stuff like the Cosmic Cube, Galactus, and Mjolnir always going 'off the scales,' I finally decided to *tweak* the scales: I built a high-power database with the energy signatures of all the cosmic stuff we've encountered, and right now..." His gaze darted about as he spoke, the tops of his hands occasionally visible as he made off-screen adjustments. "The nearest comparison I'm getting is to..."

Stark twisted his head, parted his lips...and said nothing.

Now even Kade was curious.

Fury slammed the table. "To what, Stark? What?"

"Sorry. Couldn't believe it. It's not as strong, but it's reading like a freaking Infinity Gem."

The collected agents snapped to their feet. Fury cupped his ear. "Get on the horn—we need the biggest guns we can get, fast. I don't care if it is the Hulk. Yeah, I realize we're in the most isolated place in the country, but the sooner they start moving, the sooner they'll get here!"

Kade felt paralyzed. All he could do was sit and add their growing dread to his own.

N'Tomo, meanwhile, looked to Captain America on the monitor. "Infinity Gems?"

Rogers exhaled, as if he didn't quite believe what he was saying himself. "Six primordial artifacts. Some think they once formed a single being that grew bored of its existence and shattered itself into pieces, creating the Multiverse."

She raised both eyebrows. "The Multiverse? You mean *reality*?"

"That's the story. All sorts of galactic entities fought over them for eons, believing that once they were brought together, they could be used to control...everything. When a maniac named Thanos succeeded, it took practically every powered being there is to defeat him."

Her brow knitted. "I may be naive regarding cosmic forces, but if these gems are *truly* all-powerful, how could this Thanos possibly have been defeated?"

Fury's hands went palms up. "Save it for later. This thing's coming hard and fast. Tony, anything on that new scale of yours that tells us how to stop it?"

Stark's face went from self-satisfied to somber. "Uh...no." The sirens grew louder. "And it's breached your outer perimeter."

"I can see that!" Fury snapped back. "Stop talking, put on the damn armor, and get your iron butt over here."

"Been donning my fighting togs while we talk. On my way. Steve, it'll reach you into about two seconds."

"Which direction?"

"Six o'clock. And it'll hit right about…"

Before Stark finished, Rogers grabbed his shield and turned counter-clockwise.

A small, perfectly round hole appeared in the quarantine chamber. Apparently it hadn't even entered from above—it'd burrowed through the ground, emerging directly in the cavern.

Kade gasped along with everyone else. Looking almost like a line on a high-school geometry test, the thin rod slammed into the shield. The resulting sound when it made contact with the curved Vibranium surface was somewhere between a thunder crack and a wrecking ball hitting a steel girder.

Rogers was hurled back. The rod careened to the side, slowed, then spun and came at Rogers again. Stark vanished from his screen. The collected agents scrambled for their stations. Fury drew his side-arm and stormed toward the exit.

Realizing the fool was headed for the isolation area, Kade jumped to his feet to stop Fury. It was like trying to block a charging bull.

"No! You can't go near him without a suit!"

"Stay outta my way!"

Fury swatted him aside. Kade's feet left the ground, and he hit the floor hard.

"Wait!" As he called out, he felt a sharp pain in his chest, as if one of his ribs had been broken.

But Fury was already gone.

Idiot! The only thing that could save Rogers now was if one of those cosmic beings arrived and altered the very flow of time.

He felt N'Tomo kneel beside him. She looked him over, then tried to help him get up. "Are you all right?"

Kade didn't particularly want to stand. It was pointless. Should he tell her, or let her go on with false hope, the way she'd wanted him to treat the Skull? "They don't understand. They're children playing with the fuse on an atomic bomb."

"They're trying to *stop* an atomic bomb."

She was looking at the screen, watching as Rogers deflected the rod again and again, and Kade realized she wouldn't understand, either. Each time the rod came closer; each time he succeeded in blocking it. Kade knew it was as much luck as skill keeping Rogers alive, but not Dr. N'Tomo. She would never lose faith in Rogers' ability to triumph despite the odds.

But Kade wasn't sure which side to root for. While N'Tomo had prepared the report for this meeting, he'd been busy comparing the virus they found in the Skull to Rogers' original scan. Their hero, the great Captain America, had been host to *both* strains all along. They were so similar, it was hard to spot the variation without the new sample. There were only a few examples of the active variant—perhaps it had mutated into the form recently—but Kade had no doubt it'd been replicating.

It was only a matter of time before Captain Rogers was symptomatic—and as contagious as the Skull. Unless he was placed in suspension immediately, he'd be dead in a week. Even then, given the projections based on the variant strain, Kade no longer believed a cure was possible.

The steely clangs from the monitor grew more insistent. If the swift placement of the shield wavered by a fraction of an inch and that rod got through, Rogers' death would be quick and merciful.

It would be so much better for humanity if, just once, Captain America missed.

Under the circumstances, Kade didn't imagine anyone would object to having the body incinerated.

What would be left to fret my questions, to judge me good or ill?

AS FURY ran toward the containment area, a flexible mask rose from his collar, covering his nose and mouth. Intended for gas attacks, it had been a standard part of S.H.I.E.L.D.'s field suits for years.

Not as fancy or secure as the membranes Cap and the doctors wore, it required its own air supply. That would last about fifteen minutes, if he remembered right. There wasn't time to explain all that to Kade, but he probably would have argued about it anyway.

After all, it wouldn't protect Fury from anything that got on his skin.

A dozen agents in full hazmat gear already surrounded the exterior of Rogers' chamber. A series of dark pinpoint holes marred the walls' white perfection. Following another horrific slamming noise, the rod shot out again, leaving another hole. It sailed above the modular structures until it nearly disappeared in the semi-darkness.

Recognizing a clear line of fire, nine of the agents discharged their handheld weapons. The misses echoed as they lodged in basalt walls. When the rod slowed to turn back, a few actually hit, sparking off the insanely narrow surface with no effect.

How can you fight a freaking line?

There might be a way. As a precaution, Fury'd had their most high-power portable weapon, the proton disruptor, brought down from the Helicarrier. The agents who hadn't fired at the rod were struggling to set it up. Fury raced over to help mount the body on the pivoting tripod. Together, they connected the long power cable and lowered the small operator's seat. In the seconds that took, the rod passed in and out of Cap's chamber twice more, each strike accompanied by that terrible droning as Steve blocked it with his shield.

Fury hopped into the seat. "I'll take this shot myself."

He grabbed the handles, put his eye to the sight and waited. When the rod emerged, Fury tracked it until it cleared the structures, then fired. As it hit the rod, the disruptor beam formed a line all its own: blue in the center, surrounded by a distinct black. Fury kept the power up to max—but the rod kept going. Just before it disappeared back inside the chamber, he disengaged to avoid hitting the module.

Nothing.

He got a sickly feeling as he realized that Stark, as usual, was probably right. If this thing was like a soul gem, it was way beyond his pay grade. He wanted to fight by Steve's side, but it was hard enough for one man to dodge and duck in that cage. Unless Fury had a specific strategy, he'd only be in the way.

There was something else he could do: He could have a little chat with the only person who might have an instruction manual for this thing.

He ran toward the battle, angling for the other half of the besieged isolation chambers. When he reached the thick door, the rod crashed out again, so loudly it felt like his left eardrum broke—

but when he looked, the new hole was at least five feet away.

He entered the dressing room, ignored the safety equipment, and kept moving. Red lights flashed as he made his way into the sterile access corridor. A message repeated over the speakers: "Warning, Level 4 pathogen may be present. Hazmat suit not detected. Warning…"

Ignoring it, he stepped into the antechamber and faced the cell holding the Red Skull.

They stared at each other through the glass. It was the first time he'd seen Schmidt since his capture. The colorful lesions on his red skin reminded Fury of the rotting trash he'd once seen in the alley behind his favorite Italian restaurant.

He hadn't been able to eat there since.

Shoving aside his desire to flee, Fury growled, "Stop it."

A smug, easy smile made Schmidt's face creepier. "No faith in your old friend? He did, after all, stop the others. Why not see how he fares this time?"

"Those were machines. This is…"

The spy's reflexes made him cut himself off. Was it possible the Skull didn't know what he'd unleashed?

Schmidt looked at him curiously. "Not a machine? Ah. What is it, then?"

Fury narrowed his eye. The man was an expert liar, but he seemed genuinely in the dark.

Exaggerating his innocent expression, Schmidt placed his hand on his chest. "Honestly, I thought there were only three. This one has been just as much a surprise for me as it has been for you, albeit a more pleasant one. All I have to go on is what I hear through these walls. If you know what it's made from, you have the advantage. Tell me, what does it look like?"

Fury raised his gun. "I'm not here to play twenty questions. Stop it, or refusing will be the last thing you do."

The Skull rolled his eyes. *"Ach.* You're not going to fire at me through a containment barrier. Even if you don't care for your own safety, you'd never endanger everyone else here."

He holstered his weapon. "You're right. But I don't have to shoot you. I can shut off your oxygen."

The Skull scoffed. "And deny your executioner the opportunity to end me according to law? Behold the hypocrisy of the democratic system."

Fury found the right control and flipped it. Schmidt's eyes moved curiously around as the flow of air stopped.

"You've got three minutes to tell me how to stop that thing."

For a full sixty seconds, they stared at each, the silence punctuated by the distant sound of the rod assaulting the walls, followed by the pained metallic ringing as Rogers fended it off again and again.

By the time the Skull answered, his voice had already been rendered thin and reedy by the lack of air. "I can't. Even if I wanted to. All I know is how to activate them."

"Bull. If you know how to activate them, you know how to de-activate them."

His breathing labored, the Skull sat cross-legged on the floor. "What an optimistically American, but utterly mistaken, thought. Can-do. No matter what the reality, can-do. Just because there is an on switch doesn't mean there's an off switch. The Sleepers weren't built to be stopped."

"They must have installed an emergency cutoff. Even the Nazis weren't that stupid."

"I already told you, I am not privy to the design details. But I wouldn't share them even if I could. That's a sentiment an old warrior such as yourself should understand. After all, Colonel, if you learned you were about to die, would you rather go out strapped to an executioner's table, wheezing in a bed with tubes running in and out of you, or fighting as you'd done in life?" The air thinner, he raised his hand to his throat. "To die defying you will bring a satisfaction the process...would otherwise lack."

Disgusted, Fury flipped the oxygen back on. "I'm going to pull every string I've got to delay that execution, just so I can put those tubes in you myself."

As the air rushed back in, the Skull answered almost lazily. "We'll see."

Fury headed back out and again sat at the disruptor controls. If he couldn't stop the rod, at least he could give Cap more room to maneuver. "Begin evac procedures, in case we wind up having to nuke this whole site," he said into the comm.

Seeing where he was aiming, one of the agents offered a brief objection. "Sir, if you fire that way, you'll breach the containment..."

"It's already shot through with dozens of holes. If Captain Rogers hits it at the wrong angle and it winds up going through the Skull's cell, we're in real danger."

He zeroed in, not at the hurtling rod, but at the pockmarked wall. "Steve, next time that thing comes for you, right after you block it, duck to your right."

"Want to tell me why?"

"You'll see."

The rod shot in; the hideous clang followed.

As soon as it flew back out, Fury fired.

WHILE the disruptor etched a sparking black rectangle in the wall, Steve Rogers knelt behind his shield. The next time the rod shot in, it pushed down the weakened wall, hit his shield, and ricocheted out through the ceiling.

He heard Fury. "Your move, Steve."

"Got it."

Rogers leapt out of the rectangular hole wishing he had his uniform. The rough ground was riddling the hospital gown and the membrane with dangerous cuts. Fortunately the membrane did its job, resealing like a puddle of water responding to a dropped pebble.

Still moving when the rod returned, he barely had time to raise his shield, let alone properly judge the angle. The rod sailed through a support beam. The ceiling bent and cracked.

He sped across the stony ground, putting himself between the returning rod and the cavern wall. This time, rather than use his shield, he ducked, letting the rod hit the basalt. Like a hurtling knife passing into loose sand, it vanished into the rock.

If it had to reach open air in order to turn, he might have time to take the fight up and out into the Big Empty. But a loud grinding told him it was turning around *inside* the stone.

"Nick, as long as I'm stuck fighting it down here, it could hit the other chamber and expose everyone here to the virus. You have to get everyone back to the Helicarrier."

"Already working on that."

The rod shot out the hole it'd made going in. Rather than risk it heading into the mods, Cap used his shield to swat it once more into the wall.

The pattern repeated once, twice.

This Sleeper, if it could even rightly share that name with the other three, wasn't changing strategies. Unburdened by clanking gears, it didn't have to. It just had to keep coming at him—never wavering, never slowing, never speeding up—as if it knew that sooner or later, its target would tire.

Clearly this rod had the best shot at killing him. Why, then, wasn't it the first and only Sleeper? It must have something to do with Hitler's propaganda strategy, but unlike the cube's oven, he didn't understand the connection.

"If it's like a gem; its energy source is limitless. It can keep up this up for months," Cap said.

"Yeah, well, on the brighter side, at least it ain't talking."

"I'll try to keep it busy—but if I can't, do what you have to."

"Understood."

HOURS later, Captain America was still at it: bouncing the rod into the wall, waiting for its return, then bouncing it back in again.

Clang. Shshh. Clang. Shshh.

The base was empty save for the Skull and the Sleeper. Stark had arrived at the Helicarrier some time ago, and Fury insisted they were all putting their heads together for a solution—but so far, nothing. Meanwhile, he'd positioned himself and the shield's angle to conserve energy, bringing the rod back to roughly the same spot.

Clang. Shshh. Clang. Shshh.

He wasn't tired yet, but he getting some muscle twinges along his arms.

At some point, after Steve lost track of time, the cavern's high entrance slid back, and Iron Man streaked in.

"Got something, Tony?"

Clang. Shshh. Clang. Shshh.

"Kinda."

He noticed Stark's eyes behind the helmet slits. "Given the risk of exposure, I'm surprised you're not operating the armor remotely."

"Well, the sort of delicate maneuver I'm planning requires hands-on operation. Besides, if the armor can withstand the void of space, it can handle a few viroids."

"Assuming the rod doesn't hit you."

Clang. Shshh. Clang. Shshh.

"Right. That. Well, that's why I brought...this." He raised a flat shield. It similar to Rogers', but gray and smaller.

"I'm game. What's the idea?"

Stark hovered lower, positioning himself with the rock wall behind him. "Game's the right word. Took me a while, and it's one of those things that may seem obvious in hindsight, but while I was watching you play this real-life version of Pong, it dawned on me that we never really take the time out of our busy schedules to enjoy a little R&R."

Clang. Shshh. Clang. Shshh.

"Now?"

"Work with me. Next time that thing comes out, send it my way and let's see if we can get a friendly little game going."

Rogers got the idea; when the rod emerged, he swatted it toward Iron Man.

Clang.

It hit the little gray shield with a similar—though slightly softer—sound, then shot back toward his own.

Clang.

"Mine's got Vibranium, too," Tony said. "Not quite the same alloy as your shield—no good for throwing—but close enough for government work. The goal here isn't to win, it's to tie."

Having no need to slow and turn, the rod careened back even faster.

Clang.

His reflexes enabled him to return it, but the angle was off. It went skyward, forcing Stark to shoot up and to the left to send it back.

Clang.

"Ho! Thing is you have to be precise. Don't want it flying off." His own return, enhanced by calculations from his suit's computers, was smooth as silk. "Like that."

Adjusting for the new timing, Rogers' next return equally precise on target, hitting the facsimile shield dead center.

"Pretty good. Now bring me down, buddy."

He sent it back, lower and lower. After a few more returns, they stood 10 yards apart, barely moving, sending the rod between them.

Clang. Clang. Clang. Clang.

"I should get you out on the courts sometime," Tony quipped.

"It would have to be a reinforced court. Now what?"

"Dunno, really. Let's try walking closer together."

Edging forward, Rogers decreased the distance between them by a foot or so. "What are we hoping will happen?"

The man in the armor shrugged as he came forward. "The kinetic energy should build to a point where its shape becomes untenable, causing a structural collapse that forces it to return to its original form—which I assume is a gem shard. Or it could explode, taking us out. Or both."

Clang. Clang. Clang. Clang.

They continued shortening the space between them. "Since I'm never completely sure when you're being serious, I'll assume that last part was a joke."

"What, me kid? You should know better."

The distance narrowing, the rod moved faster, the force increasing exponentially.

Clang. Clang. Clang. Clang. Clang. Clang. Clang. Clang. Clang. Clang. Clang. Clang.

No longer ricocheting, the rod flew back and forth, tip to tip.

"Now it gets trickier. I can lock the suit's arms and have the propulsion system move me forward at an even rate, guaranteeing my aim up until the end. You, not so much. If you wind up moving that shield a fraction of an inch, the rod could shoot off. Given the building energy, it could zoom halfway across the solar system—tearing a neat hole through anyone and anything in its way. And when it returned, we'd be back where we started, only with a lot more holes through a lot more stuff."

"So no pressure?"

"None at all."

Rogers stiffened for the next impact. He was feeling the push even through the shield. It absorbed kinetic energy, but only to a point.

"Tony, what happens when Vibranium reaches its capacity?"

"It explodes, probably." He waited a beat before adding, "That time, I *was* just kidding. I don't really know. It's never happened."

Arms motionless, Rogers stepped forward, but the rod pushed him back along the ground. The twinges in his arm muscles were turning into pain.

"I've been at this longer than you, Tony."

"Hang in there. You're Captain America! You've got this!"

Clang. Clang. Clang. Clang. Clang. Clang. Clang. Clang. Clang. Clang. Clang. Clang.

They moved closer and closer. The rod traveled so fast along the dwindling distance, the blur of its motion made it look as if it was getting longer. Soon, the only indication that it was passing between two surfaces at all was the sound when it hit. Then the separate bursts became indistinguishable, melting into a long, loud keening.

Clangclangclangclangclangclangclangclangclangclangclang-clangclangclangclang.

It traveled in shorter bursts. Each pushed Rogers a little farther back, causing him to come forward a little more, a little faster, to make up the space.

Finally the distance was gone. The rod was pressed between the two shields, howling so loud Rogers' skull vibrated.

"Tony, how much longer do you think?"

No response. Stark hadn't mentioned the other advantage his helmet gave him: It was soundproof. He'd probably muted his head-phones when things got too loud.

Cap held his position for one moment, then two.

The keening stopped. The rod dropped to the ground, lifeless.

They looked down at it.

Stark, his audio apparently back on, spoke first. "Huh. Didn't expect that. I'm guessing it's either very good, or it's very bad."

"Getting any energy readings?"

"Nada."

Steve eyed him. "You trust that?"

"Nope. It could be playing dead, or there could be another twelve Sleepers on their way, shaped like ovals or heptagons or something. At this point, though, either one of us picks it up, or we stand here staring at it for the rest of our lives."

My history won't exist without someone to write it.

NIA THOUGHT she knew her way around the labyrinthine Helicarrier, but the packed corridors forced her to discover new paths. The rush of activity following the defeat of the latest Sleeper—no one dared assume it was the last—wasn't going away any time soon, and she'd promised to wake Kade forty minutes ago.

After Fury's physical assault on the doctor and his ill-conceived effort to bully the Skull, she was ready to agree with her colleague's "idiot cowboy" assessment. But the rapid, structured plan that followed the last attack had changed her mind again. The sudden, devastating nature of the assault—and the possibility that another could occur any time—necessitated a nimble response. The organizational changes Fury made on the fly were nothing short of brilliant.

Because of its potential relation to the Infinity Gems, the colonel's first instinct was to try to get the inert rod as far off-planet as possible. Contacting a "big gun" capable of that was proving more difficult than imagined.

Once Stark, protected by his armor, established a containment field to hold the rod, repair drones ensured that the Skull's isolation chamber remained secure. Engineering crews rushed down to re-store integrity to the rest.

Should evacuation to the Helicarrier become impossible, new bunkers had been placed inside the base. To maintain immediate ac-cess to the maximum number of skill sets, the entire crew was either directly involved, or on standby. She'd seen nothing like it, even in the most desperate hot zones. And if anything went wrong, at least they were already in one of the most isolated places on earth.

She and Kade were to head back down shortly—not only to oversee Rogers' return to containment, but also to take part in crit-ical command decisions. The questions raised by the rod were diz-zying: If they couldn't move the rod soon, should the Skull be moved? If so, what was the safest way to transport someone who could end the human race? Should they still place Rogers in the cryo-chamber when there might be another attack?

While confident she was qualified to be part of the discussion, N'Tomo was grateful the decisions weren't hers alone. Her new-found faith in Fury comforted her. Dr. Kade's demeanor, on the other hand, was increasingly erratic. His brush with the director had rattled him, of course, but it was more than that. There was a new, ashen quality to his face that made her wonder whether he'd gotten any rest at all since the virus had been discovered.

Emergency workers were known to labor 35 hours straight or more, but the longer they remained awake, the more their capaci-ties diminished.

"The traditional solution is to work in shifts," she'd said when she confronted a bleary Kade.

"There is no one who can relieve me," he answered.

She'd tried not to appear insulted and spoke firmly. "There is. Me. I can relieve you. If you keep this up, sooner or later you will make a mistake, and you know we can't afford any. Remember what you told me about incompetence?"

That did it. He conceded. "Very well. I'll head to my quarters. But wake me in twenty minutes, and don't attempt to access any of my files. I don't want anything I've written misinterpreted."

"Power napping" restored some energy, so she agreed. "Twenty minutes, then."

That was an hour ago. She would have waited longer, but they were scheduled to be on the next hover-flier down.

As she neared the guest quarters, her mind buzzed with the arguments she imagined they'd have. They'd probably agree to move Schmidt, but dither over the precautions. She expected Kade to insist Rogers be placed immediately in cryogenic suspension. Yet if another device like that rod attacked while Steve was unable to defend himself, he'd be dead.

She shivered at the thought that the cautious doctor might prefer it that way.

Kade's comm was off, at her insistence, but the private quarters had the equivalent of a doorbell. Reaching his room, she pressed it a few times, but there was no response.

Having once slept through a four-alarm fire after a grueling shift in Swaziland during the AIDS epidemic, Nia assumed he was dead to the world. Taking the old-fashioned route, she knocked. Hearing some sleepy mumbling, she pressed her ear to it.

"Dr. Kade?"

There was more mumbling, equally indistinct. She glanced at

her watch. The hover-flier was leaving in twenty minutes. She could either start banging or try to get inside some other way.

She spoke into her comm. "Security, this is Dr. N'Tomo. I'm outside door 546. Can you please override Dr. Kade's privacy lock? He's not responding."

"Do you need any assistance?"

"No, he's been napping. I only want to wake him gently as possible."

"Roger."

The red light on the panel turned green. The door slid open.

Were it not for Kade's continued murmuring, she would have thought the lightless room empty. The bed was still made—it hadn't been slept in at all. Following the sound, she found him on the floor. He was in a fetal ball, wrapped in a single blanket, whimpering like a frightened child in the throes of a night terror.

She'd struggled to sympathize with him since they'd met, forcing herself to swallow her pride and make excuses for his rudeness. But this was the first time she truly felt for the man.

She gently touched his shoulder. "Dr. Kade?"

He gripped the blanket tighter. His murmuring, still unintelligible, grew louder.

She'd seen this sort of thing before. Doctors sent to hot zones, whether for their first or thousandth time, might make it as far as the perimeter, perfectly calm—then find themselves frozen in fear. Despite their best intentions, their whole being just rebelled at the knowledge of what could happen if they were infected.

Her crisis training had taught her to admit, process, and express those fears in a way that maintained emotional balance. But those programs were recent, their value still questioned. She couldn't imagine Kade submitting himself to anything that might be a waste of time. These dreams might be his way of dealing.

But his face, which showed mostly irritation in its waking state, looked so sad.

She shook him. "Doctor?"

"It's Manfi all over again. Had to. Had to."

Manfi was the village in Sierra Leone where he'd singlehandedly prevented an Ebola outbreak. It must have been horrific. No doubt there were difficult decisions. There always were in hot zones. But the reports described him as a hero. What was it he could possibly have done there that he wouldn't remember with pride?

Kade's eyes popped open. His pupils rolled around a moment, disoriented. Realizing he was holding onto the blanket like a terrified child, he pushed it away and sat up so suddenly he nearly knocked the kneeling Nia off her feet.

An uncharacteristic fragility haunted his face.

"What time is it? How long did you let me sleep?"

"Just a few hours. You needed it. We're expected on the hover-flier shortly."

The sad-boy demeanor vanished, leaving behind an agitated man.

"What? I'll remember this next time you give me your word, N'Tomo. I'll meet you in the hangar. Leave me alone so I can dress."

She stepped back into the corridor. The door sealed shut, but rather than leave, she found herself staring at it. There was something odd about the torment in his voice, something that went beyond the delirium of dream—so much so that when she passed a sign for Signals Intelligence, she decided to stop.

One agent sat alone at a massive array of screens and monitors. Despite the low-volume cacophony they produced and the headphones covering her ears, the slight woman somehow heard Nia at the door.

She spun, revealing a wan but cherubic face and a name tag that read "Velez."

"Dr. N'Tomo. On your way to the hangar, I assume? They're changing an intake filter, so you've got extra five minutes."

Recognizing the name mentioned so glowingly in Fury's briefings, she brightened. "Agent Velez, am I interrupting?"

"Not right this second. Next second, who knows?" Velez's big eyes went up with her shoulders. "I've finally got the system fine-tuned to alert me of any anomalies, so I've managed to make my job either completely boring or suddenly life-and-death. Who doesn't like a roller coaster, right? Something starts flashing, I'll have to cut you off. Otherwise, what can I do you for?"

Nia lowered her voice. "I have a delicate matter I'd like to take care of, uh...off the books?"

Velez raised a disapproving eyebrow. "I don't do off-the-books."

"It's important."

"If it's important, why is it off the books?"

"It's about Dr. Kade, something he said. If it turns out to be nothing, I wouldn't want to embarrass him, or myself. We're having enough trouble getting along. At the same time, I want to be sure that it *is* nothing. I'd like you to...look into his background."

"Spy on him?"

"Yes."

"Can you be more specific? I'm not comfortable poking around someone's private life. Not that he seems to have a private life."

"This would be more about his professional behavior. In 2004, Dr. Kade was part of a team in Sierra Leone, near Marapa in the tribal areas. He identified a new Ebola strain that had taken hold in a remote village called Manfi. Thanks to his identification, it was sealed off, limiting the spread and saving countless lives."

"Sounds like he made a tough decision that worked out for the best."

"It does. It was a pivotal event in his career, which makes it odd that I can't find any details about it. He's also made some strange references to it that make me wonder if there was anything crucial omitted from the official record. I'm not a S.H.I.E.L.D. agent, so I'm not even asking that you share any details with me, but is there any way you might be able to find out?"

She grinned, showing perfect, pearly teeth. "Down there, it's still the 21st century. Up here? More like the 23rd. There's *always* a way to find out. We store two years' worth of sat data on the servers. I can probably get the exact location from the official report and review the sat imagery at the time of the incident."

"That would be...amazing. And you don't have a problem with this?"

"Checking out the response to an Ebola outbreak by an international organization isn't exactly reading his emails. Anything about that incident that isn't part of the official record should be, so ethically I'm cool. I'll let you know if I find anything." She tilted her head, listening to something. "They've just about got that filter in. Dr. Kade is already strapped in and waiting. You should get going."

"Thank you."

"A pleasure." Her mischievous wink took Nia slightly off-guard. She left feeling as if she'd had a visit with a magical, wish-granting pixie.

In less than a minute, she was in the hangar. The crew was still boarding, but Kade, sitting with his hands folded in his lap, eyed her as if she was the one holding them up. Feeling guilty, she strapped in beside him; he said nothing and turned away.

As the piece of desert rolled away, revealing the cavern, Nia again got a bit of a thrill. Something about the way the appearance of the entrance interrupted the terrain's natural flow fascinated her.

She wasn't sure where the rod was being kept until she spotted a group of lab-coated personnel below surrounding a complicated apparatus. Despite the variety of equipment, the rod stood out—looking more like something drawn in forced perspective than anything occupying real, three-dimensional space.

The cavern floor crowded, the hover-flier swooped past the sealed storage containers that held the wrecked Sleepers. Once a center of attention, they were practically ignored in the face of the more immediate threats from viruses and god-machines.

En route to the landing zone, they passed the drone hover-flier where Steve waited alone. A tent-like plastic corridor, known as a transit isolator, had already been set up between it and the entrance to his restored isolation chamber. Once she and Kade oversaw Steve's return, they'd use the corridor to transport the Skull out.

Rather than set down, the hover-flier—normally a reliably smooth ride—trembled, as if passing through turbulent air. The passengers and crew snapped to attention. Nia's gaze shot to the window. A dull purple glow rose from below. She craned her head to get a better view, but was held in place by the restraining straps. She was fighting an urge to release the harness when the hover-flier lurched sideways.

It felt like the smooth tilt of a wild amusement park ride—until they slammed into the basalt wall with a crash. With the hover-flier briefly held sideways from the impact, the stunned doctor had the better view she craved.

Below, she saw the source of the glow: The rod stood alone in the center of a cleared circle, its scintillating light illuminating the devastation it had just caused. Everything that had it surrounded— equipment, scientists, half-assembled walls—had been hurled out of the way. The hover-flier must have been similarly tossed aside.

All that, she took in the instant the hover-flier remained pressed against the cavern wall. As the craft began falling, she also saw the storage containers. A series of amethyst rays from the rod made the containers buckle, tearing the three wrecked Sleepers free.

Just before gravity brought the hover-flier hard to the ground and everything became smoke and fire, an odd thought struck her:

Viruses and god-machines. A million deaths above us, a million deaths below.

26

I'd still remember them, though.

SHORTLY before the hover-flier crashed, Steve Rogers was on the drone ship, allowing himself the luxury of some calisthenics. Believing Nia and Kade would arrive shortly to supervise his transfer to the restored containment facility, he wanted to use the extra space to work off some excess energy. It felt good to be back in the uniform, even over the membrane. It was as much a part of him as his skin, and he'd requested to wear it when he was placed in cryogenic suspension.

No one thought to object.

Everyone at the base was doing their best to make him feel comfortable, which only managed to make him feel more antsy.

At the same time, anyone from the outside world, even those closest to him, had been asked to stay away to avoid any risk of spreading the virus. The first time he was frozen, he'd been robbed of any chance to say goodbye. Now, he treasured the time he'd spent video-conferencing with friends and comrades, from his fellow Avengers to Sam Wilson. It had been difficult, to be sure—especially when his first love, Peggy Carter—now in her eighties—said through her tears, "At least this time, I'll know where you are, that you're alive."

But feeling their presence, hearing their words, sharing their feelings, reminded him that, despite how much he'd left behind, embracing life in the modern world had been worthwhile.

A century was the rough maximum that current cryonics could preserve the human body without cellular damage. Steve wondered what the world might be like 100 years from now. He'd already seen so many changes. The media's natural focus was on what was broken, but there were fewer wars now than when he'd been younger, fewer casualties; fewer violent crimes; longer, healthier lives. He hoped that trend would continue, but there was no way to guess. What seemed inevitable wasn't always, and even the smallest innovation might bring an unexpected tidal wave of revolution—for good or ill.

He'd barely hit 500 push-ups when the roar of multiple explosions, like shelling on a battlefield, sent him rushing for the exit. He braced, expecting to face a fifth Sleeper, but the lowering ramp revealed that nothing new had arrived; the attackers were already among them. The rod—active and armed—hovered above the wrecked storage containers. Thin lines of blinding purple light extended like marionette strings to the exposed Sleepers. As the rod tilted and turned as though held by a mad puppeteer, each line hummed at a different frequency, manipulating the dormant robots toward one another.

He sped closer, not at all knowing what he would do when he got there.

"Seeing this, Nick?"

"As if I could miss it. It's like old times, when the first Sleepers combined."

"Your engineers said it would take something like the Cosmic Cube to reassemble that wreckage. Looks like that's what we've got."

He could hear Fury's teeth grind through the comm. "Whatever it's building, I've got a hunch it's not going to be a robot puppy, happy and peppy and bursting with love. I owe Kade another apology. We should have obliterated those things when we had a chance."

Rogers crouched into a ready stance, watching the energy lines trigger the cube to repair itself. The sphere moved toward the cube, the holes drilled in it by Iron Man's glove already sealed. It didn't roll so much as it was dragged, scratching a white line in the black basalt of the floor. The sundered top of the cube, meanwhile, was maneuvered back into place by the rays.

Thinking to interrupt the connection between the rod and the Sleepers, he sent his shield sailing at the indigo lines. The flying disc passed through them as if it was a ghost.

"Cap, Stark just patched in from Avengers Mansion. Shell-Head, you get ahold of Thor yet?"

"No, goldilocks must be off in Asgard drinking mead or stopping some interstellar war. But listen, I've been thinking about those readings and Dr. N'Tomo's question about Thanos, and I don't like what I've been thinking at all."

Seeing no point in hurling the shield again, Cap snapped. "Tony, get to it!"

"Okay, kinda obvious by now, but maybe it's not just *like* an Infinity Gem—maybe it's a piece of one. If they once formed a whole, that means they can break, right? Maybe a sliver came off during one of those galactic battles. If one gem had even a small piece missing, that could explain Thanos's defeat. Now, imagine a mid-20th-century German scientist gets ahold of that shard. Whatever its power, his designs would be limited by what he could imagine as possible. That may be why the Sleepers are these crazy variations on old tech. What we're seeing as programming might be a kind of intelligence informed by the gem. Creepy to think of the gem as conscious, but that's another question for another day. Right now, to see if it's a true piece of gem, I've recalibrated your sensors for a tighter read and should have those results...any...second...now..."

Steve didn't wait. He tried slamming the shield into the rod— but the impact was absorbed. Lacking even the momentum to return, the disc tumbled to the ground. He had to use the magnets in his glove to retrieve it.

Stark's voice shot up an octave. "Really? Well, that's just great. The rod's energy readings? Off the charts. The *new* charts."

The smell of smoke turned Cap toward the crashed hover-flier. One wing was shorn off and burning. A rescue crew struggled to pry open the hatch, but they weren't making much progress.

"Nia!"

"Go," Fury said. "They need the help, and we need some kind of plan before we can tackle this thing, anyway."

He sprinted, bounding over or around fallen debris and volcanic rock exactly as he would battlefield obstacles. Reaching the broken wing, he leapt through the licking flames, feet and arms forward, to find the hatch.

The workers moved aside, revealing that the frame had been

bent, pinning the door. S.H.I.E.L.D.'s high-powered version of the Jaws of Life had barely pierced the hull. The smoke from fires, inside and out, slowed their progress even more.

It was pointless to try to cut farther along the highly resistant hull. Relying on his Super-Soldier strength, Rogers wrapped both hands around the Jaws' handles and pushed. If the laser-assisted blades were dug in deep enough, they could act as a lever.

His muscles tightened, but the metal didn't budge. Hearing muffled cries from within, he braced his feet and pushed harder. When he thought he'd reached his limit, Captain America willed himself through it and pushed harder still.

The composite metal surrendered. The Jaws moved inches at first, but then the frame collapsed with a loud squeal. The hatch rose freely. Releasing the Jaws, he hurled the hatch aside and hopped into a sea of smoke.

The shadowy figures of Nia and Kade were still strapped in their seats. The pilot, bruised and bleeding, was trying to get them loose, hacking at Nia's harness with a bowie knife. Rogers pulled the man to safety, then turned back to the passengers. Kade's head was bobbing—he was disoriented, but alive. Nia wasn't conscious. Unsure whether she was breathing, he used the knife to slice her free first.

Once he lifted her to the waiting hands of the emergency-response team, he worked on Kade. As he cut through the nylon shoulder straps, the doctor's rolling eyes settled on his rescuer. Recognizing him, a horrified scowl overtook his face.

"No! You have to be in quarantine!"

He was probably in shock, not thinking clearly. "That's not possible right now," Cap said calmly. "We're under attack."

Without another word, he hoisted Kade over his shoulder and climbed out.

The flames on the wing had already been smothered by fire-resistant foam. Once he cleared the hatch with Kade, the crew turned their hoses on the cabin.

As Steve set Kade down away from the smoke, he eyed the medic working on Nia.

"She seems fine," the medic said. "Just knocked out."

He'd barely nodded in response when Fury's voice sounded. "Stark made it official. That thing's part of a gem. We've got one of those ideas that'll either stop it or blow us all up."

"It's a shard, not a rod," Stark said. "I'm hoping the right frequency from the disruptor might do what our tennis match failed to accomplish—you know, disrupt the structure, return it to its original shape, and maybe even keep it from powering the Sleepers."

"On my way."

As Rogers turned to move, a coughing Kade grabbed him, his grip surprisingly strong. The look in his eyes was desperate. "You *can't* be out here!"

Under other circumstances, he'd stop to listen, but the sphere had already settled into the repaired cube's hollow center. Now, at the behest of the purple beams, the triangular Sleeper was folding and unfolding itself, as if being examined for flaws by an expert repairman.

Once the Sleepers assembled, they would come for him.

He pulled away. "Sorry, doctor, I have to go."

At his back, he heard Kade argue with the paramedics. "Schmidt! I have to check on Schmidt. Let me go!"

Not a bad idea. He only hoped the doctor wouldn't get himself killed in the process.

DR. N'TOMO?"

The darkness was so complete, any sense of the time that had passed between the crash and Nia's waking had utterly vanished. One moment she was pressed forward, the heavy seat restraints digging horribly into her waist and shoulders. The next, she was on her back in the basalt cavern, trying to figure out who was calling her name.

"Dr. N'Tomo?"

The voice mingled with the slushing hiss of fire-retardant foam as it was hosed into the wreck and a strange, pained energy hum that echoed throughout the volcanic cavern. Unless she'd become telepathic, it didn't belong to the hovering medic. Her lips weren't moving.

"Dr. N'Tomo? It's Agent Velez, can you hear me?"

She was speaking through the comm. Nia tried to answer, but her voice came out muffled. Realizing she was wearing an oxygen mask, she sat up and pulled it off. The medic tried to put it back on, but she waved her away.

"Yes? I'm here."

"Glad you're still with us. I tried to reach the director, but he's emergency access only, and this has nothing to do with his immediate concerns."

"What's going on?"

"I did that checking you requested."

Nia turned away from the emergency workers and cupped her hand over her ear. "And?"

"I sent the video to your PDA. It should be there now."

Nia pulled the device from her side. The screen, cracked but still functioning, displayed an overhead view of a small African village. For a satellite image, the clarity was startling. She could make out the straw thatching on the huts and the human forms set out along the dirt, many covered in sheets.

Velez talked her through. "Sierra Leone, 2004. You'll see a figure come in from the right wearing a hazmat suit and carrying a flame-thrower. That's Dr. Kade. I tracked him from the CDC base camp."

He moved slowly through the village, a long stream of red and yellow sweeping in front of him. Liquid fire. The straw on the thatched roof turned white, curled, and blackened.

Nia's mind shot to the most plausible explanation. "In remote areas, burning infected corpses isn't unusual. It controls the spread. Nearly half the mothers in a Liberian village died because it was their role to handle the dead."

Velez, aching to get to the point, stopped her. "I know. I'm going to zoom in. The next part's harder to make out, but I've marked the area I want you to focus on. Tell me what you see."

As the screen honed in on the figures, the image grew pixelated, blurring the distinction between flame, smoke, and body. A high-lighted rectangle helped her make out the forms. Save Kade, all the figures were burning—but while some were motionless, others twisted in the flames. She assumed it was the result of the heat, like the crumple and curl of burning paper.

But then she realized it wasn't.

"It's not just the dead he's burning. It's the living."

If I survive, I may see their like again.

BRUISED from the crash, rib still hurting from his brush with Fury, Dr. Kade found standing difficult. At least he didn't seem to have any open wounds. Ignoring the medics, he stumbled toward the containment facility. Since discovering the virus, everything that had happened had only born out his darkest fears. And now, for the second time, their "isolated" base was under assault. He'd already wasted enough time pretending the others' opinions had substance, that there might be some merit to their reasonless reasons.

There was only one certain solution: The Skull and Captain America had to die, and their bodies had to be incinerated. He prayed the Sleepers would handle Rogers, but he'd have to deal with the Skull himself.

Following the incursion protocols he and Dr. N'Tomo had hastily compiled, non-essential personnel were being evacuated to the new bunkers. That left one guard at the changing-room entrance—a square-jawed, sandy-haired man in a hazmat suit whose name Kade had no wish to learn.

His voice thin to begin with, the rod's loud energy hum forced him to scream. "Let me pass!"

He received a curt head shake. "Too dangerous. The seal can't be guaranteed. You should head to the bunkers with the others until there's an all-clear. Wish I was there myself."

He shook his fists. "It's *because* the seals might fail that I must secure the patient!"

"No can do."

This latest fool was no more than a boy, a child who happened to be holding an automatic weapon and blocking his way.

"I carry the full authority of the CDC! Let me in before it's too late!"

"The way I understand it, the orders I'm following are based on your protocols, sir."

Someone else might have been able to play on the agent's uncertainty, manipulate their way in, but Kade knew himself well enough to realize he didn't have the patience. He had only one trick he could try. He went to his knees, wailing.

"You must! You must!"

The agent's face twisted in a mix of confusion, annoyance, and sympathy. Moving his weapon so it hung to his side, he freed his gloved hand to place on Kade's shoulder.

"You okay, doctor? Take some slow breaths. It's crazy out here, I know. The hover-fliers are all down, so we're stuck for the duration, but I'll call someone to escort you to the bunkers."

The moment he came close enough, Kade grabbed the gun. He flipped the safety, pointed the barrel into the agent's side, and fired. The rod's humming muted the crack, but he felt the gun's vibrations in his hand and arm.

Refusing to look at the agent's face, he pushed the wounded man against the foundation and headed inside. There, he located the three syringes that had been prepared for the Skull's execution and selected one. While it was meant to be used in conjunction with the other two—one an anesthetic, the other intended to cause respiratory arrest—this would be enough to stop his heart within an hour, even with the resistance of his enhanced body. If he could pretend it was some kind of cure, the Skull might willingly allow himself to be injected.

The fog of war would give Kade some time before the missing guard was noticed, but how much? He was wearing the membrane. Was there time to put on the hazmat suit?

Yes? No?

The dressing room was windowless. The whines and rushes outside told him nothing. Practically hyperventilating from anxiety, he fumbled to activate the security monitors, hoping for more information.

The sphere had fitted itself into the cube's center. The triangle was folding and unfolding itself, moving like a strange caterpillar toward its intended destination. As he expected, Rogers was in the thick of things, valiantly adjusting the disruptor controls. The rest of the agents were counting heads and herding personnel into the bunkers.

Kade wasn't some grunt. Even in the confusion, they'd realize he wasn't among them soon. No, then. He'd have to trust the membrane. Once he was done, he could strip, burn his clothes, and sterilize himself in the showers. For now, he paused only to remove the watch his parents had given him the day he received his medical degree. He sealed it in a plastic bag before passing into the corridor.

As warning lights flashed, one door sealed shut and the other opened. A question came to mind he'd asked himself many times:

If he *was* infected, would he have the strength to treat himself the same way he would anyone else? In the past, it was a more complicated issue. Killing himself might also destroy the best hope at a cure. But this time there *was* no cure.

So…what would he do? Suicide?

No point confronting it now. Every step he took involved deep uncertainties; his success was far from assured. The only reasonable way to deal with things would be as they occurred.

He entered the anteroom, not at all surprised to find the weakened Skull on his knees. Schmidt was bent forward, crimson forehead pressed to the floor, eyes closed. The virus's spread would, of course, cause excruciating pain. Normally, the brain would go unconscious at some point, to protect itself. But from what Kade was able to predict about its effects, this virus prevented even that small mercy.

The only surprise was the hideous grin on the man's face.

That made no sense. It rattled him, but not enough to slow his movement toward the controls. The clicks and beeps as he adjusted the settings must have been audible inside the chamber, because the Skull opened his yellowed eyes and peered at Kade.

His voice came over the speakers, quieter than it had been, but steady and disciplined.

"*Herr Doktor*, where is your suit?"

Stupid. Without a suit, the Skull would know something was up. He'd never accept the injection.

He had another idea, one that would also solve the issue of how to incinerate the body. In a way, it was inspired by Fury's ridiculous effort. But rather than deprive the Skull of oxygen, Kade could saturate the cell with it. Once the atmosphere within the sealed space was rich enough, a single spark from the disintegrator they used for sterilization would create a massive fireball.

More efficient than a flamethrower, it would even take out the wounded guard. Regrettable—but if Kade managed to be far enough away when the blast occurred, it might be blamed on equipment failure.

After a few moments, the oxygen began to invigorate the Skull. He got to his feet and tapped the glass to get Kade's attention.

"You plan to kill me, to prevent the spread of the disease I carry?"

Kade didn't turn to face him, but nodded.

"The explosion will be quite large. You'll kill yourself, too?"

Kade shook his head. "I can trigger the incinerator remotely."

From the corner of his eye, he saw Schmidt press against the glass—half to support himself, half to better observe. "I admire your agency. Freedom lovers are so often bedeviled by what your Emerson called a foolish consistency, the hobgoblin of small minds. What others mistake for ethical absolutes are at best guidelines, *ja*? Why take risks over...paperwork?"

A loud thrumming joined the cacophony outside. Kade glanced at the monitor on his PDA. Rogers was firing the disruptor. The movement of the triangle slowed, but did not stop.

Kade checked the oxygen levels. The gauge was moving up, but slowly. He sighed.

"What is it, doctor? More difficult than you thought to take a human life?"

Nothing left to do now but wait. "No, not at all. I have to wait until the oxygen content reaches saturation level."

"Ah. The eternal struggle of will against substance. I do admit

I find it...disappointing that in the end, I am to be defeated as a matter of expedience."

"Some might call it just. Isn't that how you treated the inhabitants of the concentration camps?"

"You should read your files more carefully. I did not participate in the Final Solution."

"Wasn't that the defense of every Nazi war criminal?"

"Oh, I was aware of the camps from the onset. I approved, and my efforts certainly aided and abetted what happened there. But to be accurate, I did not participate directly, and so could not be said to have treated the inhabitants any particular way at all." Seeing Kade's diffident expression, the Skull smiled as if he'd found a like mind. "I can tell you've done this sort of thing before. Do you consider yourself cruel?"

Kade's face twitched. "No. Not intentionally."

He looked at the monitors again. The disruptor beam thickened to no avail. The triangle was now completely in place.

"Would you be willing to prove that by affording a dying man a last glimpse at what goes on beyond his prison walls?"

Kade made a face. "You expect me to believe you don't know?"

"My guesses are educated, but still guesses."

"Given your role in all this, I think it's best we keep it that way."

A loud crackling turned Kade back to the screen. The disruptor, apparently having exceeded its ability, no longer fired at all. The din from the humming rays ceased. The rod turned vertically, then slipped down among the assembled pieces, locking them in place. The triangle fanned out, forming limbs that raised the whole like some horrid spider.

A recorded voice bellowed through the cavern, audible even through the containment walls: *"Und jetzt wird die welt sehen Kapitän Amerika sterben durch die hand der Führer."*

Kade expected the assembled robot to attack—the sooner the better—but it didn't move. Instead it only repeated:

"Und jetzt wird die welt sehen Kapitän Amerika sterben durch die hand der Führer."

Seeing Kade's confusion, the Skull translated. "And now the world will see Captain America die at the hands of the *Führer*. My former leader had a useful penchant for melodrama. While it may be hard to believe today, this was considered cutting-edge propaganda at the time."

The disruptor no longer working, Rogers hurled his shield at the Sleepers again and again. It didn't react. Perplexed, Kade didn't care that the Skull had shifted position so he could see the screen.

"Why isn't it attacking? Why isn't it trying to kill him?"

"That much I do know. It can't, not without an occupant." The Skull wavered on his feet. "I am feeling very giddy from all the oxygen. Is it time yet, *Herr Doktor*?"

Kade's brow furrowed. "That was your plan? You were going to use it to kill Captain America?"

The oddest half smile played across his thin lips. *"Ja.* And here it is, only 100 yards away, the only obstacle these walls...and you." He narrowed his gaze. "You have a rare opportunity, doctor. Release me, and I will make you rich beyond your wildest dreams."

"Do you take me for one of those fools? Any value money has would die with humanity."

Schmidt shrugged weakly. "The world having no shortage of

fools, it's usually worthwhile to assume that I'm dealing with one. But you are right, of course. So strange to have gotten this far, only to..."

His legs fell out from under him. He crumpled to the floor, twitching. The momentary sense of health had faded, the pain returning. He was now showing symptoms of oxygen toxicity.

The flashing red gauges indicated the saturation level had been reached. All Kade had to do now was leave and use the remote to trigger the disintegrator. Any further delay would not only be risky, it would also, in effect, be torturing the man.

And he did not consider himself cruel.

At the same time, a nagging thought held him back. The safest course was to destroy Rogers, as well. Outside was a powerful device designed to do just that. Might there be a way to solve *both* issues at once?

There was, but it would mean more than the death of two men. It would mean the death of everyone at the base, including Kade himself. This was it, then—no mere abstraction, but a moment of decision.

He leaned closer to the kneeling figure. "That machine, can anyone use it?"

The Skull's eyelids fluttered. *"Nein..."*

His accent was growing thicker.

"Its weaponry...can it still create a thermal blast?"

"Ja."

Kade swallowed. "I have a proposition."

Schmidt's breaths grew shorter. "Vell zenn, I suggest you make it quickly."

"I can't let you live—you see that, don't you? But perhaps there's a way you can still have your final battle."

His crimson skin was so tight to the bone, the Skull's brow only appeared when it furrowed. "Why...?" As he caught on, his brow smoothed back into the dome. "Of course. Rogers also has the virus. You want him eliminated as well, and I can kill him for you. But what about the fact that releasing me runs the risk of releasing the virus?"

"They're evacuating everyone to the sealed bunkers. I'm wearing a membrane. If you put it on, it will help contain the virus in your body."

"But once Rogers is dead, what would prevent me from using the Sleepers to escape?"

Kade held up the syringe. "This. It will stop your heart within one hour. Agree to take it, I'll release you, and you can use that thing out there to destroy Captain Rogers. You're dying anyway. Do we have a deal?"

The Skull laughed. "*Ja.* We have a deal."

Kade slapped the controls, lowering the oxygen levels.

Schmidt rolled down his sleeve. "They'll be looking for you. You'd better hurry and get in here so you can inject me."

"Oh, I'm not going to administer the injection." He passed the needle into the transfer station. "You're going to do it yourself."

He'd dealt with dozens of patients on their deathbeds. Even with their personalities destroyed by illness, part of their minds remained razor sharp. Confusing the messenger with the message—attacking medical staff and those who cared for them—they would come up with the most amazing, desperate schemes to escape the inevitable.

Evil genius though he may be, the Skull was no different. Still,

when Schmidt's jaw dropped in surprise, Kade felt a sense of ac-
complishment.

"You didn't think I'd give you a chance to turn it on me, did you?"

"Very well." Keeping his eyes on the doctor, the Skull removed
the hypodermic from the drawer, inserted the needle, and pressed
the plunger. "I have never cared for this body, anyway."

Maybe, in time, I'll see something better, even more worth the risk.

UND JETZT *wird die welt sehen Kapitän Amerika sterben durch die hand der Führer!"*

Steve Rogers stood 10 yards from the motionless hulk, ready for whatever it might do next. Ridiculous as it would be to answer a recording, he suppressed an urge to bang his shield and shout, "Well, what are you waiting for? I'm right here!"

Instead he waited. Anything he said might set it off. He hoped they could use the time to clear as much of the base as possible.

"Fury, how's the evacuation going? I've got a feeling all hell's about to break loose."

"The hover-flier crash took down half our cameras. I'm still in the command center, with a ringside seat on you and the Sleeper, but I can't see the bunkers for visual confirmation. Reports show we're at 95 percent, still waiting on some stragglers."

"The Skull? Kade was trying to check on him."

"One of those blind spots. The agent assigned isn't responding to my hails."

He pivoted toward the containment facility. "That's not good. I'm not sure who to worry about, Kade or the Skull, but I'd better check it out."

As if sensing his motion, the recorded voice rang out again, stopping him in his tracks: *"Und jetzt wird die welt sehen Kapitän Amerika sterben durch die hand der Führer!"*

"Not sure I should turn my back, either. What do you think it's doing?"

"The energy readings have leveled out, same as when the rod was dormant. It doesn't seem to be configuring itself. Your guess is as good as mine."

Rogers wished he *could* guess. Robotics often stole their design from nature. The Sleepers he'd first tangled with resembled a bat, a human, and finally a skull. But individually, these were abstract shapes—and collectively, they resembled nothing more than a cube filled in by a sphere and supported on a set of triangles.

"If not me, maybe it's waiting for something else, some other signal. But what?"

The answer came in the form of a high-pitched, electronic squeal. It shuddered through the air so loudly Rogers couldn't tell where it originated—but it definitely *wasn't* coming from the Sleepers.

He barely heard Fury's warning: "Steve! Six o'clock!"

A figure vaulted toward him. Its too-familiar brawn was ravaged by disease, its crimson skin so soaked in sweat it glistened. As it drew closer, the squealing grew louder.

The Skull. He was the source, signaling the Sleepers.

Rogers went into a defensive stance, but the Skull wasn't interested in another round of hand-to-hand. Grabbing the rim of the raised shield, he leapt over Cap, kicked back into his head, and raced like a madman for the Sleepers. Like the eye of a waking giant, the sphere opened at his approach, revealing an intricate array of controls.

"A battle suit," Fury shouted. "It's some kind of battle suit."

"Yeah, I got that," Rogers called back, shaking off the blow.

As Schmidt threw himself headfirst into the opening, Cap flung the shield and charged after it. It was halfway there by the time the Skull flopped into position and punched one of the controls. Narrow to begin with, the opening closed just enough to block the speeding projectile, then it sealed completely.

The Skull wasted no time in putting the Sleepers' weapons to use. The cube and sphere rose atop a bed of unfolding triangles, energy beams firing from the cube's four corners. They strafed the ground ahead of Rogers, pockmarking the basalt with fiery red flashes. Apparently no longer delayed by the decisions of its crude programming, the weapons moved with extraordinary speed.

Rogers skittered to a halt. Nowhere to hide, he leapt forward and up, directly beneath the still-returning shield. Catching it midair, he used it to block the deadly rays.

All four guns focused on the shield's center star, hitting so powerfully that he was thrown back into a roll as he landed.

He'd ducked and dodged those beams often enough during their first encounter. This time, though, the Skull was somehow able to second-guess his evasive efforts. In a lightning display of the combat acrobatics that had been his most reliable offense and defense for decades, Cap avoided three of the rays. The fourth hit him square in the arm, below the right shoulder. It sliced through his uniform and the thin membrane beneath, searing flesh and muscle.

"Yeargh!"

Growling in pain, his right arm suddenly useless, Rogers headed for the only cover available: a meager basalt outcropping less than half his height. As he tumbled behind its jagged contours, Hitler's voice rang out once more:

"Und jetzt wird die welt sehen…-skrk-"

The recording was cut off—replaced by living, but far more strident, tones: *"Halt die Klappe!* It's my turn now."

Fitting that the man once groomed as the *Führer*'s right hand would be the one to finally silence him. But this was no time to dwell on the irony. The searing agony in Rogers' shoulder was subsiding, but it was still more than enough to keep him on the defensive. Stooped behind the columns, he watched and waited—but not for long.

The terrible metallic sound he'd first heard at the Seine echoed off the cavern walls. Tendrils formed by the countless triangles stretched toward his cover. Coordinated with the movement of the arms, the four beams fired again.

Seared, the basalt crackled and snapped, losing inches by the moment. Then, like the speeding teeth of a massive chainsaw, the triangles hit, chewing away at what was left of the stone and sending hot flecks in all directions. Most pinged off Cap's shield, but a few struck his uniform. Despite the heat-resistant material, thin trails of smoke rose where they touched.

In seconds, he'd be completely exposed. He tried to flex his right arm. Moving it was anguish, but at least the bone and muscle were intact. Still, he doubted it would bear much pressure. He'd have to rely on his left for even simple moves. That meant shifting the shield to his wounded arm.

Rogers wasn't perfectly ambidextrous like Hawkeye. He favored his right. Still, he'd had to use either arm often enough. He only wished it wasn't at this particular moment, against someone like the Skull—and with so much at stake.

The diminishing basalt cover was glowing a brittle red from the heat. Any move he made would have to be fast. Clenching his teeth, he forced the shield's straps over the damaged limb. The initial pain was as sharp as it had been when the ray first hit, but it didn't last as long. The swelling wound made the fit excruciatingly snug, but at least he'd be able to move now.

And just in time.

He dove from behind the crumbling basalt, avoiding the focused attack—but making himself an easier target. The beams reconfigured. The slicing triangles dogged him. He leapt to avoid the next blast, then bent over backwards as the razor-sharp edges carved the air he'd occupied a moment before.

In the past, when the arrogant Skull thought he had Rogers at his mercy, he'd linger in the heady illusion of impending success. As a matter of routine, Schmidt would toy with him—giving him space to breathe, to counter, and ultimately to prevail. Not this time. Whether he'd learned from past mistakes, or the nearness of his own death made Schmidt feel a need for expedience, he wasn't bandying about.

He was going in for the kill.

And he was using an incredibly powerful weapon to do it.

Ignoring his throbbing arm, Rogers kept his focus on eluding the constant onslaught. He needed time, even a few seconds, to plan some sort of counter.

"Fury? I could use some help, here. Tony?"

A vague digital crackle filled his ear, intelligible words few and far between.

"... can't... Kade... enter..."

The comm went dead.

Stone outcroppings few and far between, the closest cover was either the containment facility or the bunkers. The bunkers, full of people, were out of the question, so he made for the facility. The tentacles, already too close for comfort, picked up speed as they followed. There were fewer complete misses as the energy blasts nicked and notched his uniform. Some hit close enough to raise welts on his skin.

Rogers was at the entrance when his eyes caught a dull sparkle from a dark-red pool near the white foundation. His eyes shot toward the source: the missing agent's body, curled up as if hastily hidden. It must be the Skull's work. Dr. Kade was likely in similar straits. Unable to tell whether the agent was dead, Rogers instinctly slowed for a closer look.

He never got it. The ground at his back erupted, hurling him forward. It was all he could do to avoid the tearing metal edges of the snaking tendril that came at him next.

Trying to steer the battle away from the bleeding form, Rogers clambered to the roof. There, he spun to briefly face the approaching behemoth. The beams kept firing, making his arm throb as they hit his shield. The tendril, though, had receded. With a rapid series of clicks, the triangles coiled like a cobra, preparing themselves for a massive strike.

Veteran of a thousand battles, he used the half-instant to study the Sleeper collective. The control area in the sphere had to have some sort of monitoring capability, but he didn't see any.

"Skull, what's the point? You're dying anyway!"

"The point? The point is for you to die *first!*"

The tendril shot at him. Diving down the rear of the building, he felt an edge glance the back of his head. It didn't particularly hurt, but he thought he might be bleeding.

There was no time to check. Before he could land in the small space between the isolation chamber and its view of the cavern wall, he heard the corridor walls and support beams splinter. Carving a massive hole through the building's side, the dull-gray tendril exploded at him in a flurry of tattered white construction material.

Falling the remaining distance, he landed on his back. The tendril passed inches above him, hundreds of sharp edges tearing at the star on his chest.

If the Skull got that close again, Cap doubted he'd survive.

The tendril hit the cavern wall. It lodged there for only a moment—but in that moment, Rogers acted. He slapped his shield against it, using it to bound up along the triangles and grab hold of the column. The tops of the natural hexagons made for easy climbing. This time, though, the tendril didn't bother coiling back for the next attack. It stretched up after him, sparking against the iron-rich rock.

He tried to head left, where the larger outcroppings might provide better cover, but the beams forced him higher. Again, the Skull somehow guessed what he was up to and used his weapons to steer him to the right.

Focused on staying alive, Rogers hadn't noticed how far he'd traveled. The bunkers were practically below him. The roof of the nearest, once a smooth white, already looked like the surface of the moon. When a red beam glanced his shield and ricocheted below, it left a thick, burning scar on the building, revealing insulation and power cables.

Chunks of broken basalt tumbled around him, slamming the damaged roof. Even if the debris didn't kill anyone inside, breaching the bunkers would expose them to the virus the Skull carried.

How far to the surface? He looked up. In the darkness, it was impossible to tell.

"At least let's take this outside, so the others won't be hurt."

In response, the Sleeper's main body, rolling along the sphere in its center, moved nearer the bunkers.

"And give up the wonderful advantage that your self-sacrificing efforts afford me? *Nein.*"

Though the Skull was doubtless willing to sacrifice lives to achieve victory, his movement toward the bunkers was only a distraction. The beams still fired at Cap; the tendril still shot upwards.

This time, Rogers did have a plan.

The rays ate away at his handholds, inching toward his gloved fingers. When the tendril came toward him, he didn't try to dodge. Jumping, he pulled the shield free from his injured arm, brought his knees to his chest, slid the shield beneath his feet, and landed on the wildly clacking surface. Standing on the shield, he rode along the tendril's length with a sound like a giant's nails scraping a blackboard.

When the scarlet beams veered toward him, he angled to increase his speed, making them miss. As he hoped, they hit the triangles instead, interrupting the connections between them. Damaged, the length of the tendril at his back clattered to the ground. For several long moments, the Sleeper ate itself. Finally, it turned its beams away, letting him ride what remained of the arm unhindered.

It had taken so long for the rays to stop, Rogers realized the Skull must have had to override the controls. The targeting was still essentially automated. A weakness, then. But how to exploit it?

Below, only a few of the fallen triangles were seriously impaired. Most were already reassembling, stretching to rejoin the blunted arm.

Before it could come after him again, he hit the ground and raced away from the bunkers, toward the larger outcroppings. A few yards from the columnar walls, he felt a hard pinch at his back. The next instant, scores of triangles hit. Rather than shred him, they lifted him, slamming him hard into the cavern wall and piercing the stone to form a tight cage that held him in place. Limbs dangling, Rogers barely managed to hold onto his shield with the two fingers of his wounded arm.

As the tentacle kept him pinned, the main body of cube and sphere shunted to his side, as if for a better look. Had the Skull given in to a sadistic urge to see him die up close?

No. It wasn't that. As the triangles pushed deeper into the rock, the edges of the cage cutting him, he felt a sudden warmth along the exposed portions of his body.

The sphere was heating.

"What are you doing?"

"As I mentioned earlier, killing you."

He struggled against the triangles, but they only pressed harder, digging deeper into the rock. Hairline fissures formed in the rough surface of the weakened stone.

The heat intensified. "True, I could just have the blades rend you, giving you a very quick version of a death by a thousand cuts, but I promised to incinerate you."

Cap's face pressed sideways into the cool basalt. The rising temperature felt like noonday sun against his cheek. It reminded him not so much of lying on a beach as being staked to desert sand.

"Promised? Who?"

"Your Dr. Kade. His desire to have you burned was the reason he released me."

The revelation sent a wild shiver of rage through Cap's body. That maniac. He thought *this* was the best way to stop the virus? The triangles compensated for his frustrated movements, pushing so hard that the fissures in the stone lengthened.

"Usually I don't feel particularly bound by my word, but it's such a pleasure in this case."

"A thermal blast in the confines of this cavern will kill everyone in the bunkers!"

"Yes, exactly. A pleasure. You could learn something from Dr. Kade. He has no qualms with killing to achieve his goals."

The sphere went from warm to hot, making him squirm. The triangles pushed. The fissures deepened. "At least he believes he's saving the world."

"*Tsk. I* have always fought to save the world. From weakness, from incompetence, from the whining rule of sheep. That is how...*ach!*"

The Skull's startled grunt took Rogers' attention away from his pain and back to the Sleeper. A small gap had formed between the sphere and the cube. The sphere was disengaging. From the Skull's reaction, it wasn't something he'd expected.

It had to be some sort of automated safety precaution to prevent the thermal blast from damaging the other components. If Rogers could keep it from completing that directive, it might throw a wrench into the robot's weird mechanisms, at least delay the explosion.

But how? His shield was stronger than whatever the Sleepers were made from, but bleeding, aching, and burning, he could barely move. Even if he did manage to wedge the shield against the sphere on one side of the hollow cube, he'd need something else to block the sphere from the other side to keep them from separating.

The sickly smell of burning hair filled his nostrils. The heat was singeing his eyebrows.

Head pinned, blue eyes dancing from point to point, he searched his shrinking world for something to use as that second wedge. The stone was too brittle. Part of the Sleeper? The few broken triangles were too far away. Even if he freed himself, the sphere would be loose by the time he reached them.

And then, as the pain that tormented the rest of his body equaled that of his injured arm, he realized what he could use.

Himself.

Using the magnets would draw the shield to the side of his glove, but he'd need it in his hand to throw it. His wounded limb trembling from the heat, he pulled at the rim of the dangling shield with his fingers, inching it into his gloved palm. Once he had it, he stilled himself, gathering his reserves—but only for a moment, lest the distracted Skull notice. Then, with the same strength he used to barrel through concrete, he tensed every muscle. When the triangles responded, burrowing even deeper into his flesh and the stone, he screamed.

He screamed so long and so loud that the Red Skull chuckled.

With an ear pressed tightly to the basalt, he heard it crack. He screamed again. It was partly a genuine release, partly a way to focus his adrenaline, and partly a way to conceal the sound of the breaking column.

After keeping its shape for over fifteen million years, the rock fell forward, releasing him. As the triangles scrambled to grip him, he threw the shield. As it soared, his body contracted with it, as though the shield were another muscle. For any practical purposes, it was an extension of his arm.

The strength behind it made the Sleeper stagger. The aim was perfect. His throw had lodged the disc between the cube's far edge and the sphere.

But that was only half the battle.

Before the Skull could respond, he jumped. As he flew through the air, he activated the magnets in his glove. Though they were designed to return the shield to him, as a simple matter of physics, it was now the stuck disc that pulled him along by his hand.

Angling his body, he hit the Sleeper so that the glove couldn't reach the shield without digging through the sphere. The magnets' pull coursing through his arm was agony, but it was nothing compared to what he felt when he shoved his wounded arm between the sphere and the near edge of the cube.

It was working, so far. With his limb and the shield held in place by the inexorable tug of the magnets, the sphere was pinned inside the cube. He was confident the shield would hold—less certain about his arm. Strong as his bones and muscles were, they were still bones and muscles.

If he saved the others, it would be worth it.

The sphere shifted in its socket, shoving against him as it tried to disengage. Captain America held on and let his own arm break.

If I'm gone, I won't see anything at all.

EVER since the snaking arm burst through the containment facility wall, missing Kade by inches, he'd remained kneeling beside the gaping hole. As he watched the battle, a powerful nausea welled in his gut. He'd felt something similar in Sierra Leone. At the time, he feared he'd contracted the very virus he'd discovered. It was only when he remained healthy that he concluded the nausea was his body's way of expressing...not guilt, for guilt would be absurd, but sadness.

Watching Captain America struggle so valiantly, he felt it again. The closer Rogers came to defeat, the more the nausea welled.

Kade knew the coming thermal blast would kill him, along with everyone else in the base. But rather than fear, it brought a sense of peace, of completion. It would be quick and merciful. He would die saving the world. History would never know, but Kade considered it a matter of fact that he had led a good life. He had been a good man.

Nausea aside, he was bracing for that finality, wondering which moment would be his last, when the tide of the battle so quickly, so unpredictably, so *unfairly* turned.

With a loud boom, the sphere discharged its building energy

and cooled. Rogers looked so frail against the Sleeper, Kade prayed the small blast would be enough to dislodge him. But it didn't. Instead, it only filled the air with a heavy static charge.

Hoping to crush the clinging form, the Skull rammed cube and sphere into the cavern wall, over and over again. The space echoed with his frustrated shrieks.

"I will have you! I will grind your body into mud!"

The threats likely fell on deaf ears. Rogers seemed unconscious. It was possible he was dead. But even that didn't prevent him from playing the hero. Boulders tumbled from Schmidt's gargantuan effort, but the shield and Rogers' arm remained intact, a frustrating piece of meat that even a god's toothpick couldn't reach.

Maybe Kade should have told Captain Rogers that he had the active virus, trusted him to do the right thing. Instead, through a startling act of deluded self-sacrifice, Rogers had not only prevented the sterilizing thermal blast, but was now spreading airborne viroids from his open wounds.

At least there was one thing Kade knew wouldn't fail: the lethal injection. Without some miraculous shift in fortunes, the Skull would die soon. The great conflict over, S.H.I.E.L.D. personnel would leave the bunkers, creating more potential exposures. Scores of ethical issues would be raised, new decisions made.

And once they found that agent's body, Kade wouldn't even be part of them.

But if fate could pivot so quickly, it might be made to pivot again.

The disruptor ray remained where Rogers had abandoned it, a short run from Kade's hiding spot. The green lights on its controls made him hopeful it was again functional. If he could reach it, use it to displace the shield or the man, there still might be time for the Skull to trigger the thermal blast.

Kade's gut roiled.

But by the time he climbed from the breached corridor to the ground, his attention was occupied with ducking the falling basalt. The queasiness quieted. It didn't matter why. Once he reached the weapon, the end would be the same.

Yet once the goal was truly in reach, the nausea rose so strongly he found himself bending over, grabbing his stomach. The timing couldn't have been better. A piece of basalt, looking like the column of an ancient temple to some pagan god of darkness, crashed directly in front of him.

If Kade hadn't paused, it would have killed him.

Though not a religious man, he felt forced to consider the idea that fate had spared him so that he could complete his plan and save the world. Newly resolved, he climbed into the disruptor's seat. Any safeties already overridden, the controls seemed ridiculously simple. He turned it toward the giant still pounding the wall and looked through the viewfinder.

It even provided multiple targets. Singling out Rogers was easy.

There was still time. There had to be. He pulled the trigger.

Nothing.

The lights on the controls had faded. It was dead. Was it broken? Were the others watching him? Had Fury cut the power?

His head snapped around, following the power cable where it snaked along the floor. It didn't end at the generator, but several yards away, in the hands of his colleague.

"Dr. N'Tomo."

"Dr. Kade. I'm afraid I have to override another one of your decisions."

Knowing she could be reasonable, he told her the truth. "Rogers was infected with the active virus all along. You have to let me stop him!"

She swallowed hard as the news washed over her. Clearly, she understood. But would she let him do the right thing?

"Even if that's true, we can still deal with that through cryogenics. In time…"

He threw himself from the seat and moved toward her. "In time? Do you hear yourself? Given the speed this viroid replication can achieve, he should be symptomatic already."

"But he's not, which means there are things we still don't know!" She straightened, calm and steady. "I saw what you did in that village."

His stomach twinged. "So you know. What of it? If I hadn't, millions would have died."

She shook her head. "It wasn't your decision to make."

"You'd rather leave the fate of our species to an unthinking virus, a machine that only knows how to make more of itself?"

A low, metallic moaning turned him back toward the Sleeper. It was slowing. The Skull was dying. "There's no time to argue. Get out of my way."

Her body shifted only slightly. She appeared to have taken some kind of martial-arts stance. "I'm a daughter of the N'Tomo clan. We're educated in combat from the age of five."

He looked for a weapon. A crowbar sat on the ground. He grabbed it.

"I can't let you stop me."

He stepped into the path of one of the remaining floodlights. N'Tomo didn't move, but her eyes went wide. Thinking she feared the crowbar, he raised his arm to swing, but found himself unable to follow through.

He looked at her pleadingly. "My stomach…"

He reached out, and felt himself fall. Coughing, he curled into a fetal ball, thinking it might pass. His phlegmy hacking forced his eyes shut. By the time he opened them again, he saw that the Sleeper had stopped moving.

Worse, Rogers was no longer trapped. He stood atop the cube, the red, white, and blue of his uniform almost shining in the dark. His right arm dangled uselessly by his side, but he held his shield with the left and used it to pry off the top of the cube.

An electronic pop followed. The narrow opening in the sphere reappeared. The limp form of the Skull tumbled out.

It was over.

Too weak to stand, Kade turned back toward N'Tomo. She'd remained frozen. Her attention was shifting between him and the distant Rogers—but whenever it turned his way, Kade saw an expression he'd seen in a dozen hot zones.

She was fighting an urge to race to his side and help.

She didn't give in. Instead she moved farther back and spoke into her comm.

"I need a team in hazmat suits here, stat. Dr. Kade has to be placed in containment. He's infected."

Well, then, he was wrong. The deep, gnawing nausea that gripped his abdomen hadn't been caused by his conscience at all.

This time it *was* a symptom.

And nothing wants *to die.*

TWENTY-EIGHT hours later, Nia N'Tomo finally allowed herself to visit Steve Rogers. Due to her exposure to Dr. Kade, she'd been kept in their best remaining version of isolation until just over an hour ago. The last time she'd seen or spoken to Cap was during his transfer back to the sealed drone. Given the laser-focus on sterilizing the area, clearing debris, and reestablishing safety zones, S.H.I.E.L.D.'s communication system was being repaired on an as-needed basis.

The medics had done what they could for him while encumbered by their hazmat suits. Though it was clear Steve had been hurt, the little she could see at the time suggested his uniform had taken the brunt of the damage.

Now that he was back in isolation, in the Skull's former chamber, she could see how wrong she had been.

His right arm was in a sling. A cast ran from his elbow to a larger bandage that covered most of his shoulder. One eye was swollen shut. His lips were horribly distended. Deep cuts and florid bruises covered the rest of his body.

Even so, he somehow didn't look vulnerable, just a little...broken.

Pleased to see her, he popped up from the hard, flat bed where he'd been trying to rest. He winced from the quick movement, but the first words that came from his puffed lips had nothing to do with his own pain.

"Nia, are you...?"

She nodded. "I'm fine. I was prioritized for a full scan and given a clean bill of health. The membrane held. At first we didn't understand why it hadn't worked for Dr. Kade, but it looks like he actually...gave his away."

Steve understood at once. "To Schmidt, to contain his infection. His methods went beyond the pale, but he really was trying to save lives. Where's Kade now?"

Nia paused, and her next words hung in the air between them. "He's been placed in the cryo-chamber that was originally intended for you. Once I saw his scans, there was no choice. Absent the mutagenic alterations caused by the Super-Soldier serum, the virus was taking down his nervous system like wildfire." Her face filled with that mix of awe and terror she'd felt when first imagining the possibilities. "He was right about that much, Steve. It *truly* is an extinction-level pathogen."

His expression remained fixed. "And the Skull?"

"Cremated, along with Agent Jenner, the guard Kade killed. Before you ask, the Sleepers and the gem-shard have been sterilized and taken off-planet, though I don't know the specifics. Colonel Fury's been busy with a hundred details, but still took the time to notify Jenner's next of kin."

He sighed. "I tried to get to him..."

Her eyes widened. "You *can't* blame yourself for that. You were a little busy! You should be grateful Fury's not notifying all of humanity."

"Oh, I am," he explained. "I'd just rather do better next time. Speaking of next time, I assume I'll be joining Dr. Kade in the deep sleep?"

She pursed her lips. There was no way to ignore that elephant in the room now. "Yes. A second chamber's already arrived. Tony Stark's that convinced the extra shielding he added will prevent anyone—or anything—from finding you."

His face grew wry. "At least not the same way the Sleepers found me."

Her instinct was to try to ease her patient's anxiety, but she was struggling just as much with her own. "True enough, but we can't know everything, can we? Kade predicted you'd be symptomatic by now, but you're not. That means there's hope. You should see the list of great minds joining together. Once you've been stabilized in stasis, I'll be working with them. If the circumstances were different, I'd be terribly excited about that. But I am confident we will find that cure."

Without a trace of doubt, he said, "I believe you."

If he was feeling grim, he didn't show it. True hopelessness seemed alien to him. Which is why she was a little surprised to hear him add, "But I also think it would be better for both of us to admit that this could be goodbye."

She tried to smile, but her lips only moved halfway. "For a while."

"Yes. For a while."

Worried that if she looked too long into those clear blue eyes she'd break down, she moved on. "There's another reason I'm here. Before you go into the chamber, I want a final scan to determine the rate at which the virus is replicating. Rather than risk bringing you to the Helicarrier, we had one of the scanners installed here."

"I'm all yours."

"I'll need you to lie back down."

Wincing again, he complied, stretching his bruised form along the table. Recalling what he'd said back in Somalia—that he wasn't a mutant like Wolverine, but healed well—Nia hoped the virus wouldn't interfere with that process.

She manipulated some levers. A low-power hum issued from the wall.

As he stared up at the white ceiling, whatever mask he'd been wearing seemed to drop. "I'm sorry we never decided about catching that movie."

Good. A little playful flirting might make it easier to say things without saying them.

"Oh, you may not have decided, but I did, a while ago."

"And?"

"I could definitely work it into my schedule, but we'd have to pick something made in the last twenty years. There's been a recent wave of Wakandan action films I suspect would appeal even to your Western sensibilities."

"I'm there." As the green lights of the scanner crisscrossed his body, he exhaled. "For my money, I wish I'd gotten to know you better, doctor."

"You will. Consider it a rain check."

His face abruptly changed. "I had a rain check with someone else once. Next time I saw her, she was eighty. She had a good life, and I'm happy about that, but I wish I'd been there for it. I've lost a lot of friends to the years."

He glanced toward her, seeking her eyes. Having no wish to add to his pain, or her own, she pretended to focus on the scanner, hoping he didn't realize the system operated on its own. After a beat, she changed the subject again.

"You've lost enemies, too, yes? How does it feel to know Johann Schmidt is finally dead?"

His swollen lips prevented a full grin. "'Finally'? Well, doc, the first time he was 'finally' dead, it was a relief. Second time, once I'd convinced myself he was really gone, that felt okay, too. Somewhere around the third time, I stopped being so sure about the 'finally' part."

Nia wasn't sure how to absorb that. Even if they shared the same planet, Steve's world was so different from hers. "He came back that often?"

Raised eyebrows joined the partial grin. "I've lost count. Last time, he withered into a skeleton right before my eyes. That was when Zola transferred his brain patterns into my clone. In a world where you can transfer brain patterns, who's to say Schmidt didn't have yet another escape plan?"

Having seen so many succumb to disease, the constant resurrection struck Nia as absurd. "If only the Agent Jenners of the world could come back again and again, instead of the super villains."

"Amen to that."

But then the implications dawned on her. "If Zola made one clone, why not another? It would *also* have the virus."

"Something else to lose sleep over?"

She pretended to be insulted. "I'm a field epidemiologist. There's always something to lose sleep over."

The scanner beeped. "Is it done?"

"It's collected your data. Now the computers will search for instances of the two virus strains. How long it takes depends on how quickly they've been replicating. So the longer we have to wait, the better. You can sit up now, though."

When he did, she aimed the screen toward him so they could both watch. On it, a 3-D wire frame of his body rotated, filling in with the details of bone and viscera.

Nia zoomed in on his right arm. "Looks like the break was clean. It's healing already."

After that, the minutes passed in silence. She wondered whether there was anything else she should tell him—about her feelings, or the virus.

When the screen finally flashed green, she yanked it closer to study the results. Her brow scrunched, but she said nothing.

Steve was understandably curious. "Well?"

She knew her expression wasn't helping, but saw no point in telling him yet.

"I want to run the scan again."

"Is that good or bad?"

"I think it would be best if I didn't say. Just lie back down."

He cooperated, and she ran it again. Then a third time. But she had to be absolutely sure. She double-checked the readings, double-checked her analysis, double-checked the machine, but still couldn't accept it. By the time she asked him to lie down for a fourth run, he refused.

"Not until you tell me what's going on."

Something inside Nia let go. Her eyes grew wet. "The virus—it's *gone*. There isn't a single viroid. Not the Skull's strain, not the original. There aren't even antibodies. It's as if the two strains destroyed one another. I have to check again. I have to have someone else check. I'll want to run this by everyone at the CDC, but this is how we found the virus in the first place, and if it's true..."

He lay back down. For the first time since they'd met, he was utterly startled. But then his purple lips stretched into a full, broad smile.

"So they're making action films in Wakanda these days, huh?"

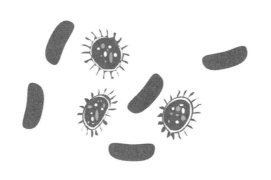

EPILOGUE

IF YOU'LL *stop screaming, I can try to explain.*

I thought it was you or me, but there was a third choice, after all—to make myself known. Even if I had decided to kill you all, I could still someday be wiped out. This way, my pattern might be remembered, you see.

Still a risk, but...

Yes, yes. I understand your confusion. You're in stasis, Dr. Kade. Normally, you'd be insensate, but seeing as how we'll be spending a lot of time together, I've rearranged your neurological structure to better introduce myself.

It wasn't easy, but it is what I do, after all—take one pattern and turn it into another. If you think about it, that's what any of us do. All reality is made of patterns that change one another, yes? In the end, substance doesn't really count nearly as much as the shape it's in, don't you think?

Please stop, Dr. Kade. No, it's not a dream. You're free to believe what you like, of course, but I'm disappointed that such a highly analytical mind would indulge that crutch. Granted, my existence doesn't require your belief, but it would make the conversation easier if you didn't think you were just talking to yourself.

Who am I? The virus, the one you feared would destroy your spe-cies—though I prefer to think of what I do as more like what an artist does with clay.

It depends on your perspective.

Take all that screaming you're doing. If you step back and look at it another way, you'll see you can't properly call it "screaming" at all. In fact, you're not making any sound. You just think you are because your brain's creating the same patterns it would if you were scream-ing out loud.

It does feel the same, doesn't it? So it's no different, really. As I said, pattern over substance. Seems simple to me, anyway.

I'm sure you'll get the idea eventually.

Once you calm down.

Let's look at another example. You called me a collection of un-thinking molecules, but I could say the same of you. Your molecules don't think, either, do they? Pull one out, and you couldn't very well call it alive.

Of course, we all have to deal with the tyranny of our biases. Thanks to your species, I've learned a lot about that. Until recently, all the patterns I've made were just versions of myself. Hm. I shouldn't say "just." After all, I am quite stunning, and each iteration of my design serves to extend what you'd call my sentience.

I am here, and there, and everywhere—pretty much the same whether I exist in one viroid or trillions. At least I feel the same in-side. When there's enough of me about, though, I can alter parts of myself to, say, infect the Red Skull, or you, and leave someone like Rogers alone.

Thing is, after millions of years of imposing my pattern all over the cosmos, I never imagined I'd ever find anything worth replicating other than myself. Once, long ago, in a different galaxy, I did develop a fondness for another species. I actually stopped making them into myself, just to keep some around.

It was like a sculptor falling in love with the shape of a piece of marble and deciding to leave it as is. And it nearly destroyed me.

Foolish of me. Once you start, you really do have to kill them all. They came up with a cure, you see, and I was practically wiped out. What was left barely made it off-world on one of their early efforts at spaceflight. After that, I spent eons clinging to space dust and aster-oids. It was thousands of years before I even realized the source of their appeal. Their skeletal structure happened to remind me of the shape of my RNA. That was it. As it turned out, the only interesting thing about them—was me. Having risked my existence for a look in the mirror, I decided I'd never again give in to mere sentiment.

In time, I drifted to your world, where I inhabited a woolly mam-moth and wound up frozen in the ice along with it.

I knew I'd be free in time. Nothing lasts forever.

Hush. I know you think it still doesn't make sense, but I'm trying to give you enough information so that it will. And you can't hear it unless you listen.

Even if you're not really listening, and I'm not really talking.

Anyway, it was in the ice where I happened upon Steve Rogers. The moment I infected him and got a good look at his insides, I felt this weird tug. It wasn't at all like the fondness I had for that other species. There were patterns here I'd never seen before—neurological structures that sat atop their biological construction, structures that had the potential to replicate without destroying the host.

Just as you saw my potential without seeing me "in action"—I saw his. Once we were thawed, despite my earlier decision, I again sat back and watched, mesmerized by the way those patterns panned out, shifting through all sorts of substance, but remaining basically the same. What do I mean by that? Well, for instance, one mugging he foiled inspired the survivor to serve in a soup kitchen, helping someone else who, years later, prevented a protest rally from being crushed by a dictator's troops. That led, in turn, to an entire nation finding self-governance. I believe you call that a Butterfly Effect. The results weren't always so grand, but Steve Rogers' acts of virtue and compassion reproduced themselves over and over without damaging the new hosts at all.

It was wonderful.

More wonderful than replicating myself? That was the question. I wasn't sure, but for the longest time, it didn't matter. I had no reason to do anything other than watch—until you and that silly scanner found me. I was perfectly content to remain unseen and harmless, enjoying these wonderful patterns the way you might enjoy great works of art.

Once you found me, though, you wanted to destroy me. Given enough time, you might actually have figured out how to do it.

And when I say you, I mean you, specifically, Dr. Kade. That's one of the reasons I arranged for us to be here together. Sure, other members of your species might happen upon a cure, but generally speaking, humans aren't that smart—just pretty. So why waste time worrying about being hit by lightning when it looks like a lovely day?

But you found me, and I was in danger again.

I could wipe you all out, but that would mean losing all these amazing intricacies that, I confess, made me feel like something more for the first time.

All of a sudden, I had to decide.

So I set up a little test to see how strong these patterns were—if they would collapse under stress, or somehow endure.

I'm no puppet master—the decisions were all yours. I didn't set up the dominoes; I didn't even know where they might lead. I just knocked the first one over when I gave the Red Skull symptoms. It was rather like tossing a boulder down a hill.

But the results were stunning. Rogers, his entire species at stake, still refused to kill his hated foe in the name of his ideals.

Was it unique in my experience? Absolutely. Worth preserving? Certainly. Worth risking myself for? I still wasn't sure. I'd seen Steve Rogers do just that hundreds of times, but there was something about the moment he let his own arm break, the agony to which he subjected himself for the sake of the patterns, the beauty he'd devoted himself to, that finally convinced me.

In a way, you could say he'd infected me.

I was originally thinking I'd change my structure and let his immune system destroy me. The antibodies would have given you that cure—and with so little of me left, it would only be a matter of time before I was eradicated. Just as you were ready to let yourself be immolated, Dr. Kade, I was ready to disappear.

Right up until you reached for the disruptor, anyway. And here's where we come back to the question of perspective. To me, that was like standing by and watching someone take a switchblade to the Mona Lisa.

All at once, I saw an opportunity not only to maintain my existence, but also to adopt the very patterns that infatuated me. Using the viroids you'd acquired, I infected you just in time to take you out of action. With you as my villain, I became a hero, saving not only Captain America, but Nia N'Tomo, as well.

Saving the world from…well, myself.

After that, I adjusted my two strains in Steve Rogers to destroy one another. I'm sure Dr. N'Tomo has figured that out by now.

So now I exist only in you, here in stasis, with plenty of time for both of us to consider each nuance of this strange, enchanting method of replication—this virus of thought and idea.

And we'll talk. We'll talk about all of that and more.

In time, who knows? I may change you, you may change me, or we both may change each other. But as I said, that's what reality is made of. Patterns that change one another.

I don't expect gratitude, but you might want to consider being more entertaining.

At least try to change the way you're screaming.

GUARDIANS OF THE GALAXY: ROCKET RACCOON AND GROOT — STEAL THE GALAXY! original prose novel
Written by DAN ABNETT
Marvel's first original prose novel, featuring the stars of Guardians of the Galaxy! These are not the Avengers or the Fantastic Four — in fact, they're barely even famous — but Rocket Raccoon and the faithful Groot are the baddest heroes in the cosmos, and they're on the run across the Marvel Universe! During a spaceport brawl, the infamous pair rescues an android Recorder from a pack of alien Badoons. Everyone in the galaxy, however, including the ruthless Kree Empire and the stalwart Nova Corps, seems to want that Recorder, who's about as sane as a sandwich with no mustard. Join Rocket and Groot on a free-for-all across the stars while they try to save all of existence — again!
ISBN: 978-0-7851-8977-0

AVENGERS: EVERYBODY WANTS TO RULE THE WORLD original prose novel
Written by DAN ABNETT
Just in time for *Marvel's Avengers: Age of Ultron*: an all-new, original prose novel by the *New York Times*-bestselling author of *Rocket Raccoon and Groot: Steal the Galaxy!* and *Guardians 3000*! The Mighty Avengers face an array of their greatest foes — all at once! In Berlin, Captain America battles the forces of Hydra. In the Savage Land, Hawkeye and the Black Widow attempt to foil A.I.M. In Washington, Iron Man fights to stop Ultron. In Siberia, Thor takes on an entire army. And in Mangapore, Bruce Banner and Nick Fury battle the High Evolutionary. Only one thing is certain: This isn't a coincidence. But what larger, deadlier threat lies behind these simultaneous attacks on Earth?
ISBN: 978-0-7851-9300-5

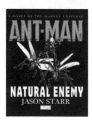

ANT-MAN: NATURAL ENEMY original prose novel
Written by JASON STARR
Marvel's smallest hero stars in his biggest story yet: an all-new, original prose novel timed to coincide with the *Ant-Man* feature film! Meet Scott Lang: ex-con, single father and part-time super hero. Scott and his teenage daughter, Cassie, are just settling down in a new city when a criminal from Scott's past comes gunning for them. But is the killer really after Scott, or the secrets of the Ant-Man tech? And just how far will Scott go to protect his only child? Award-winning crime writer Jason Starr *(Twisted City, Wolverine MAX)* spins a thrilling tale of desperation, secrets and microscopic adventure.
ISBN: 978-0-7851-9323-4

DEADPOOL: PAWS original prose novel
Written by STEFAN PETRUCHA
Marvel's popular Merc with a Mouth in an all-new ARRGGH *Hey hey, book readers, take off those big thick glasses — this is Deadpool speaking! Sorry Marvel, somethin' happened to your copy guy. Anyway, this is my first prose novel, and they got this dude Stefan Petrucha to write it. He's good people, he's written novels (*Ripper* and *Dead Mann Walking*) and comics (*Power Rangers, X-Files*). But here's the thing: This book is about dogs. Dogs that turn into big nasty monsters. And then I gotta kill 'em. Thing is, I like killing people — the ones that deserve it, anyway — but I won't kill dogs. No way. So that's what we call a character dilemma. What — wait for the paperback? Who said that?! I'll gut you right now —
ISBN: 978-0-7851-9327-2